'Let us endure an hour and see injustice done.'
A.E. Housman

4/93

The Battle of Beirut

Michael Jansen

The author is donating all royalties from
this book to the Education Fund of UNRWA,
the United Nations Relief Works Agency.

The Battle of Beirut

Why Israel Invaded Lebanon

Michael Jansen

South End Press, Boston, MA

First published in the USA by South End Press,
302 Columbus Ave, Boston MA 02116 in 1983.

The Battle of Beirut was first published by Zed Press,
57 Caledonian Road, London N1 9DN in 1982.

Copyedited by Anna Gourlay and Roger Hardy
Proofread by Robert Molteno and Roger Hardy
Typeset by Jenny Donald, Jo Marsh, and Lynn Papworth
Cover design and maps by Jacque Solomons
Cover photo courtesy of George Nehmeh, UNRWA
Text photo credits: Al-Safir (Beirut), Associated Press
(London), Gamma (Paris), Rex Features (London), and
UNRWA (Geneva).
Printed by Krips Repro, Meppel, Holland.

ISBN: 0-89608-174-5 Hb
       0-89608-173-7 Pb

Contents

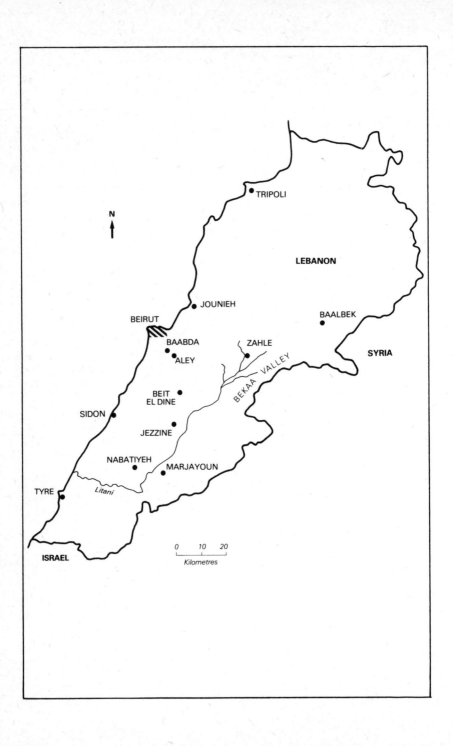

N

TRIPOLI

LEBANON

JOUNIEH

BEIRUT

BAABDA

ALEY

ZAHLE

BAALBEK

SYRIA

BEKAA VALLEY

BEIT
EL DINE

SIDON

JEZZINE

NABATIYEH

MARJAYOUN

TYRE

Litani

ISRAEL

0   10   20

Kilometres

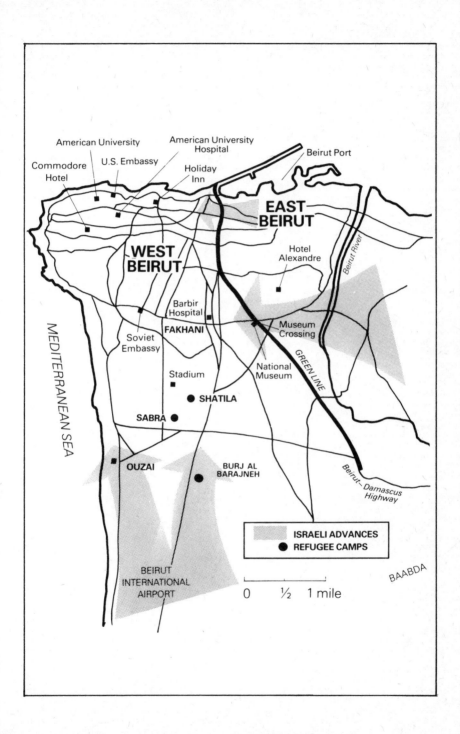

This book is not an instant history of Israel's fifth war. It is a study, and an indictment, of what the Israeli military juggernaut did to the inhabitants of southern Lebanon, Lebanese and Palestinians, as it rolled northwards to Beirut and then what it did to the citizens of Beirut. Accordingly it does not, for instance, deal with the fighting between the Israelis and the Syrians. It is a story of great destruction and much misery. I have tried to put this tragic picture into a frame by describing the military doctrine of the operation, the opposition to it inside Israel and the support given to it by the Reagan administration; finally, I evaluate its success or failure and explore the motivation behind the whole operation.

Sources:

Al Fajr, East Jerusalem
Al-Hamishmar, Israel
Al Nahar, Lebanon
Al-Quds, East Jerusalem
Associated Press
Baltimore Sun, USA
Chicago Sun-Times, USA
Christian Science Monitor, USA
Davar, Israel
Filistin al-Thawra, Lebanon
Financial Times, UK
The Guardian, UK
Ha'aretz, Israel
Ha'olam Ha'zeh, Israel
International Herald Tribune, Paris
Jerusalem Post, Israel
Kivunim, Israel
Kol Ha'ir, Israel
Le Matin, France
Le Monde, France
L'Orient, Lebanon
Monday Morning, Lebanon
New Outlook, Israel
New York York Times, USA
The Observer, UK
Reuters
Sunday Times, UK
The Times, UK
Wall Street Journal, USA
Washington Post, USA
Yediot Ahronot, Israel

1. A Famous Victory: Israel's Assault on Lebanon

Seldom has any military operation been so well publicised in advance as the Israeli assault on Lebanon. From about February 1982 onwards detailed scenarios, complete with maps indicating the probable line of the Israeli advance, began to appear in journals round the world. But all of them made the same mistake; they 'fought' the next war more or less on the lines of the last one.

The predictions did not go beyond an extended re-run of the earlier Israeli invasion of southern Lebanon in 1978. This time it was expected the Israelis would attack in much greater strength and advance as far north as Damour, the last major Palestinian base just outside the Beirut area.

When they got there, it was generally believed, the Phalangist forces in Beirut, showing gratitude for the $100 million-worth of assistance given them by Israel, would advance south to cut off Beirut in a combined pincer movement.

The predictions did not allow for two things – the larger political ambitions of Begin and Sharon, and the ingratitude of the Phalangists.

These partially-correct predictions were not the product of prophetic powers. All they did was to extrapolate and draw deductions from the open display of Israeli military strength along both sides of the southern border-line. The motivation was equally clear and open, as explained by Robin Wright (*Christian Science Monitor*, 18 March): the Israeli moves were 'an attempt to bait the Palestinians into provoking a confrontation in southern Lebanon . . . the Israeli provocations may be an effort to justify an attack the Israelis cannot afford to make because of unprecedented international pressure.'

By February Israel's planning for the operation had been under way for eight months. It was time to get some of the troops into position. So from February-March onwards an armoured division, plus motorised infantry brigades, perhaps even two armoured divisions – at least 25,000 men in all – were moved up and kept in the border area. At times, when the opportunity to strike seemed favourable, they were put on alert and moved forward; at others, they were stood down and moved back, but never out of the frontier operational and command area. These 25,000 troops would, of course, have been only the vanguard of the main expeditionary force.

In mid-January the Israelis annexed the Golan Heights. The divided Arabs huffed and puffed but did nothing. That inaction under great Israeli provocation was what, perhaps, convinced the Israelis that it was safe to go ahead with the Lebanese invasion. Soon after began a whole series of Israeli military provocations in southern Lebanon.

On 20 January troops of Unifil, the UN force in southern Lebanon, reported that Israeli forces, illegally deployed in the south, had used tanks and considerable small arms fire in training manoeuvres which Unifil described as 'intensive, excessive and provocative'. PLO troops nearby did not respond.

On 8 February a convoy of 32 buses entered Lebanon from Israel, carrying between 600 and 700 well-armed troops. They advanced close to PLO positions, which did not react; this demonstration was described by the Israelis as 'a recreational trip'.

On 8 March a much bigger force of 500 military vehicles moved up to the strategically situated village of Khiam; once again the PLO did not respond and the Israelis pulled back. Having failed three times in January-March to draw the PLO into action on the ground in the border area, the Israelis in April and May resorted to heavy aerial strikes in the south and in Beirut which, on the third attempt, finally produced the desired result: the PLO shelling of northern Galilee on 4 and 5 June.

On 30 May the Israeli Chief-of-Staff, General Eitan, in a well-publicised speech to a school gathering in Tiberias, gave the clearest indication so far of Israel's intentions: 'only a military operation can give us peace. It is not true that there is no military solution of the problem of the terrorists.'

A report in the *Jerusalem Post* (30 June) revealed that the general had expressed the same belligerent intentions in a talk given a week earlier, on 24 May. The fluency with which he expressed himself indicated that he had made the same speech, unreported, several times before. Thus, by the end of May, plans for the Israeli attack into Lebanon were ready, the determination to put them into effect was well established, and the forces with which to do so were ready to move.

Any comparative estimate of the PLO and Israeli forces confronting each other in southern Lebanon is a study of total military imbalance. In most of its earlier wars Israel had been able to maintain and project the myth of the Israeli David bravely facing up to the Arab Goliath. This had been particularly true of the 1948 and 1956 wars. The myth had begun to wear thin in the highly successful 1967 war, which revealed the volume and technical superiority of Israeli weapons. The myth was partly restored by the inconclusive stand-off of the 1973 campaign. It was totally destroyed by the quantity and quality of arms deployed by Israel in 1982.

In the Israeli media there has been a self-satisfied debate on whether Israel is now the third or fourth military world power. In the Lebanon invasion the Israelis outnumbered the PLO fighters initially in the first two or three days, by six or seven to one, and subsequently by 10 and then 12 to one.

June 1982: Israeli forces enter southern Lebanon (AP)

A detailed breakdown of the PLO order of battle (given in the *Jerusalem Post*, 7 June) said that 'PLO forces in southern Lebanon number 6,000 armed men, about half of the PLO's total strength in Lebanon. According to Israeli military sources the terrorist concentrations include a string of heavily fortified positions each housing a platoon-strength force' (a platoon usually numbers 20 to 30 men). 'Only a few of the terrorist positions are in villages.'

According to the Israelis, there were 500-700 PLO troops in the Unifil-controlled area (200-300, said Unifil); in Fatahland 1,500; 1,000 around Nabatieh; in and around Tyre 1,500; between Tyre and the Zahrani River 700. The Israelis hailed the capture of the Crusader castle at Beaufort, an 'impregnable' PLO strongpoint, as a major victory, but according to their own accounts it was defended only by 'between 30 and 50 men'.

As regards equipment, the Israeli military sources estimated that the PLO had about 35 T-34 Soviet tanks, of World War II vintage, 'and a large number of artillery pieces, including 130mm cannons, 160mm mortars and "Stalin organ" multiple Katushya launchers, anti-aircraft guns and ground-to-air Sam-7 missiles.' That is the complete Israeli tally of the equipment of the PLO ground forces in southern Lebanon. Of course, the PLO had no airforce and no naval craft.

The Israelis had 172,000 men in all, rising to 400,000 when reservists were mobilised, which they had been; 3,500 tanks, equivalent to the combined strength of the German, French and Italian armoured forces; 4,000 armoured personnel carriers; nearly 1,100 artillery pieces including 175mm self-propelled guns and 156mm and 203mm self-propelled Howitzers; and 602 combat aircraft.

Israeli military censorship prevented any reporting from Israel on what proportion of this huge arsenal was actually employed in Lebanon. Unifil counted 100 tanks and 100 personnel carriers in the spearhead that advanced up the coast road on the morning of 6 June. Robert Fisk (*The Times,* 21 June) reported 'several hundred Israeli tanks' being brought up towards Beirut with 'a mass of tanks and heavy artillery pieces stretching for more than 20 miles and filling the beaches and banana plantations'.

A more precise picture of the Israeli order of battle, from the receiving end, was given in an Associated Press despatch from Beirut on 23 June. This estimated that Israel had deployed

> 9 armoured divisions with 90,000 soldiers. In addition Israel has 1,300 tanks, 12,000 troop and supply trucks, 1,300 armoured personnel carriers, 350 ambulances and 300 buses to carry prisoners . . . Nearly one-third of its tanks and most of its regular army . . . experts say the force is far larger than is needed to overrun the 10 square-mile West Beirut enclave.

In that enclave were 8,000 PLO fighters, 1,200 Syrian troops and perhaps 2,000-3,000 Lebanese militiamen.

As regards quality of equipment there was no comparison between Israel and the PLO. Since 1948 the US has given Israel $14.9 billion in military aid, about a third in outright grants, plus grants of $7.15 billion in economic aid for the same period. So Israel could afford to buy the latest and best US weapons: 85% of Israel's planes were American, including 120 of the latest F-15s and F-16s; half of its tank force was from the US, comprising 650 M-48s and 810 highly advanced M-60s; 90% of Israel's artillery was American. Both the Israeli army and airforce relied heavily on US missiles. It was sophisticated American electronics in the F-15s and F-16s, in their super-sensitive Sidewinder and Shrike missiles, and in the Hawkeye surveillance and battle-controlled planes, able to track 300 enemy aircraft 250 miles away, that enabled the Israeli airforce to shoot down 79 Syrian aircraft for the loss of one of their own and to destroy the Syrian missile batteries in the Bekaa Valley.

Israel's campaigns are the testing ground for new American weaponry not yet used in combat by the Americans themselves. Indeed, so close is the link between Israel's insatiable need for more and newer US arms that the left-wing Israeli publicist, Uri Avneri, makes a good case for his claim (in *New Outlook*, June-July 1982) that 'if Israel did not exist the American industrial complex would have to invent it'. It is American money given to

Israel that is used by Israel to buy weapons from the American arms industry, funds that the US Congress would be reluctant to grant to the US Armed Forces. Not least among the arms supplied by the Americans to the Israelis were the terror weapons — cluster bombs, phosphorus bombs and shells, airburst bombs and shells and, possibly, the vacuum bomb.

Just because the disparity between Israel and the PLO was so obvious, the Israelis, in the second week of the war, began putting out stories about the seizure of enormous stores of arms hidden away by the PLO: the quantities, according to Sharon, were 'incredible'.

The stories of the PLO arsenals aimed at two propaganda targets: it was 'proof' not only that the Palestinians at some future date were going to attack Israel with enormous strength, but also that they were going to call in even larger foreign forces, including the Russians, for whom these weapons were being pre-positioned. The first version of the story, given by senior Israeli army officers to Jewish fund-raisers from abroad, was that enough arms had been seized to equip one million 'terrorists'; 500 large lorries would have to work for months to remove this mass of material, valued at $5 billion.

In a letter to *The Times* (2 July) Shabtai Rosenne, described as an Ambassador-at-Large, made the claim that it would take 80 lorries a whole month to transport 4,000 tonnes of ammunition, besides 140 tanks and other military vehicles, 12,500 light weapons, 520 heavy weapons, etc.

Moshe Arens, Israeli Ambassador to the US, spoke of 500-600 heavy artillery pieces being captured. Begin claimed that the captured weapons were enough for five divisions, or 60,000 men. Then, at an exhibition of the captured arms, a Logistic Corps Brigadier said, on 28 June, that the weapons were sufficient, not for five divisions, but for five brigades, or 20,000 men; and that it would take 1,000 men and 150 trucks another month to complete their removal. Clearly Israeli officials had not collated their figures. Visitors to the exhibition were told that the Russian T-62 tanks on display were a selection of the 500 tanks captured from the Syrians and the PLO.

It was left to the military correspondents of the Israeli newspapers, and notably Ze'ev Schiff of *Ha'aretz*, perhaps the best informed of them, to cut this story down to size. Schiff concluded that the weapons found were enough for one lightly-armed infantry division; that is, for 12,000 men. Altogether 38 T-34 tanks were captured and

> it is likely that some of the 46 T-55s captured belonged to the
> terrorists, but there is another view that they all belonged to the
> Syrians. So it is not true that 400 or 500 tanks were captured in
> terrorist territory. The only weapons found in large quantities were
> different types of rifles: some 10,000 Kalachnikov assault rifles . . .
> while the numbers of artillery pieces seized were also large it was not
> as great as some political leaders claimed early in the war.

(The two ambassadors had said between 500 and 600 heavy guns.)

> Fifty-one heavy guns were captured including two old French 155mm guns and 32 Russian 130mm guns, and 240 other types of artillery, some of which could have belonged to the Syrians. The booty was also poor in the latest-type Katushyas, of the 26 captured only 15 were the latest type. [Schiff concluded] Did these arms threaten Israel's existence? They did constitute a danger of raids, shelling and terror, but in no sense a danger to our existence. The strength of an infantry division with partial support is no danger to Israel's existence, unless we suddenly desire to ignore the strength of the IDF.

Giving his overall estimate of the PLO arms and forces Hirsh Goodman wrote (the *Jerusalem Post*, 9 July):

> What were found were mainly the weapons of the terrorists . . . not of an army . . . to call the PLO an army or even an army-in-the-making which could hope to pose a real threat to the Israel Defence Forces in structured warfare, would be pushing the matter to absurdity.

There were demands in the Knesset for an inquiry into the origin of the inflated claims. Because the debates were all in Hebrew they have had little impact abroad.

One of the essentials of Israeli military doctrine in its earlier wars has been the strategy of the indirect approach. Liddell Hart, the British military theorist who defined this strategy, was warm in his praise of the Israeli army's use of this type of advance: never to attack prepared positions frontally but to hit the enemy's weak spot from an unexpected angle, to get round obstacles rather than to overcome them. It had been possible for the Israeli army to do this because the terrain of its previous campaigns favoured it — the empty spaces of Sinai, the not-very-heavily populated uplands of the Golan, and even the West Bank in 1967, where the towns did not resist and could be bypassed.

In southern Lebanon, because of the terrain, the disposition of the population and the sheer size of the Israeli force, the indirect approach could only be partially applied. It is true that on the first and second days of the war the Israeli army advanced swiftly, swerving round Nabatieh, Tyre and Sidon. But while this movement looked impressive on the map it did nothing towards disposing of the enemy.

This was because the PLO fighters, while they were guerrillas, were not rural guerrillas, they were not maquis or partisans living in and off the country-side: they were urban guerrillas entrenched in Nabatieh, Tyre, Sidon, Damour and Beirut — and in the refugee camps adjacent to these towns, camps that had become built-up towns. They could not be left there, behind the advancing Israelis, because these towns and refugee camps sat astride the main coast road and the Israelis were tied to the roads, particularly to the coast road, because of the mass of their tanks and armoured personnel carriers and self-propelled artillery: off the roads the going was too rough across Lebanon's steep rocky hillsides.

So the towns had to be reduced by old-fashioned siege methods. But the usual siege methods are slow and long drawn out; even in World War II the siege of Leningrad, of Stalingrad, of the Channel Ports, had lasted for weeks and months. The Israelis were in a hurry. So they decided to reduce the southern Lebanese towns and the other centres of resistance, the camps, by smashing them and their defenders into the ground, using the tremendous firepower that they had readily available.

Hence the destruction wrought on these targets by the concentrated and combined bombardment from Israeli planes, naval vessels, artillery and tanks. The targets were drenched with fire and steel. Inevitably, civilian casualties were horrendously high. An Israeli parachute officer (*Davar*, 25 June) recorded:

> In the fire force we used we took no risks. We usually operated in a co-ordinated manner with all the means of fire we have. One of the questions that will have to be answered is: what was the justification for the use of such fire force against the enemy? I have no answer.

The need for speed, for the usual brief lightning campaign was partly military, partly political, partly psychological. When asked why the IDF should attack, General Eitan replied quite simply, 'Since I have built an excellent apparatus by the investment of billions of dollars, I must make use of it' (*Yediot Aharnot*, 14 May). This was three weeks before hostilities began.

The political necessity for speed arose from the fact that Begin had told his Cabinet colleagues, the leaders of the Opposition and the Israeli public, who began to question the purposes of the war 36 hours after it began, that it would take 72 hours at most (one report says that Begin's prescribed time was 48 hours; the *Jerusalem Post*, 8 June).

On the psychological plane, when Sharon was asked the reasons for the attack, one reason he gave was that, nine years after the 1973 war, there was a whole generation of Israeli soldiers who had no experience of battle and who needed to be given it.

There was also an important personal, human reason for the Israeli tactic of massive bombardment of inhabited built-up areas: the need to avoid Israeli casualties.

But there are only two ways to reduce a besieged city: to breach its defences and storm in with troops in street-to-street and hand-to-hand fighting, which is very costly in casualties; or to sit outside the besieged town and pound it to pieces. Naturally, the Israeli generals, with massive fire-power at their disposal, chose the latter. Israeli troops, moreover, had no experience of urban warfare. Despite their heroic reputation, the individual Israeli soldier, even the paratrooper, had little stomach for hand-to-hand combat.

So the Israelis smashed down Tyre and Sidon for several days and West Beirut for several weeks. When eventually the troops went into Tyre and Sidon, they still had to take on the Palestinians hand-to-hand amid the rubble. This was such a nasty surprise that the Israelis held back from assaulting West Beirut, preferring the tactic of 'static fire' which on 25 July the Israeli Cabinet, by a narrow majority, adopted as the official tactic to be used on West Beirut.

Israeli reaction to the use of massive firepower and massive civilian casualties, so as to avoid Israeli casualties, is well expressed in a letter to the *Jerusalem Post* (28 June):

> I vehemently protest the IDF policy of risking our soldiers' lives in hand-to-hand and house-to-house fighting. I strongly suggest that we use air strikes and artillery barrages to destroy enemy strongholds. The world always has and always will condemn us no matter what 'precautions' we take in these matters. Therefore let us protect our sons' lives first!

The writer's anxieties were both ill informed and unnecessary. But they signify acceptance, if not approval, of the tactic of mass bombardment.

Other Israelis have condemned it. Professor Porath (*Ha'aretz*, 25 June) said:

> The heavy bombardments, the enormous destruction and the high number of casualties among the refugees and the Lebanese population were supposed to make it easier for the Israeli army to occupy the area with a low number of casualties. Thus an immoral act was done: in order to lessen the number of our casualties our government was prepared to cause heavy casualties on the other side, including civilians, even Lebanese, who are not a party to the war between Israel and the Palestinians . . . Thus a most horrifying moral principle was established: Jewish blood is worth more than any other blood.

An Israeli soldier outside Beirut told Robert Fisk (*The Times*, 17 June): 'And for us, I guess, I hope you understand this, the death of one Israeli soldier is more important than the death of even several hundred Palestinians.'

Many journalists covering the Israeli attack, even those basically sympathetic to the Palestinian cause, have criticised the PLO for bringing on the Israeli bombardment of Lebanese towns and Palestinian refugee camps by siting their military installations and gun positions in residential areas or near mosques, churches, hospitals, schools, embassies. Stories have been reported of local inhabitants telling the PLO to take their fighters and their guns away so as not to attract Israeli bombardment.

These criticisms are not altogether logical. Where the PLO deliberately took up positions near such places — and there are some well-authenticated observations of this being done — then its actions were to be condemned. But, as regards the military use of the refugee camps, where else would the PLO have had security for training its fighters, the storage of its arms and ammunition, and the siting of its command headquarters?

Some of these were, indeed, sited outside the camps, but always near them and only on a limited scale, because of the opposition of the Lebanese government and Lebanese public opinion. The PLO strongholds could only be situated in areas under its independent control, and the only such areas were in the camps; whether they should have been allowed to acquire such extraterritorial status is another question.

The Israeli airforce, equipped with the very latest photo-reconnaissance and surveillance devices, had complete command of the skies over all of Lebanon, and it kept especially close watch on the southern half of the country. For this reason the PLO fighters could not function as guerrillas in the countryside; without cover they would have been immediately spotted and attacked by Israeli planes. As mentioned above, the Israeli military estimate was that in the countryside the PLO units were of platoon size only. But the larger concentrations of the fighters, from 500 to 1,500, were all in the towns, the only places giving cover from air attack. These towns were also the home ground of the fighters, many of whom had been born in Lebanon and stationed in the same Lebanese town for years on end; they had obtained some sort of employment and had settled there with their families.

When the towns were surrounded and came under bombardment because of their presence there, should the Palestinians have left the built-up areas, moved to the open fields outside and fought a pitched battle with the vastly superior Israeli forces?

The urban guerrillas of the PLO, trapped in the towns within the first few hours or days of the war, had only two alternatives: to fight and die, or to surrender. Rejecting the latter, their choice made inevitable the destruction of the towns, since the Israeli generals, in their turn, chose long-range bombardment rather than sending in their troops.

When the Israeli army moved into built-up areas, in the suburbs of Beirut or in the Achrafiyeh district of East Beirut, it did exactly what the Palestinians had been doing. It sited its artillery and tanks, its headquarters and supply depots, among civilian residential buildings because there was nowhere else to put them. A large tank park, with its fuel depot, was placed just below the Lebanese President's palace in Baabda, and that civilian establishment was targeted and hit because of the Israeli military concentration alongside it.

This writer, on Sunday 11 July, witnessed an Israeli artillery piece, sited within 100 yards of the Hotel Alexandre in Achrafiyeh, which joined in that day's heavy bombardment. Similarly, early on in the battle of Beirut, the large and conspicuous secondary school in the village of Chweifat, overlooking Beirut airport, was taken over by the Israelis as a headquarters and barracks, despite the vigorous protests of its owners.

Over and over again, as so often in its earlier wars, the Israeli army provided examples of its own peculiar interpretation of a ceasefire. The normal military practice is that when two sides agree to a ceasefire that automatically means a standstill; the troops remain in their positions. Not so for the Israelis. Under their doctrine of 'improving positions', their troops keep moving forward during a ceasefire, cautiously and without shooting.

Thus for the Israelis, a ceasefire is a continuation of the process of gaining territory, by peaceful means. When the other side observes that the Israelis are not standing still, and in order to stop them opens fire again, the Israelis loudly accuse them of breaking the ceasefire. They were very ready to declare unilateral ceasefires, especially when they needed to rest and consolidate. The PLO was then more or less obliged to match this peaceful gesture. Then the refreshed and reinforced Israelis edged forward and the PLO was obliged to break the ceasefire.

The Israelis achieved a major goal, the encirclement of Beirut, by 'improving positions' after the first ceasefire of Friday 9 June, just as they took over all of the Metn area, in central Lebanon north of Beirut, during the tenth ceasefire.

This went hand-in-hand with the Israeli policy of concocting breaches of the ceasefire, a policy so systematic that it provoked a joke in the Israeli army (Hirsh Goodman, *Jerusalem Post*, 28 June) 'about the idiot in the ordnance corps who must have put all Israeli cannon in back to front: "each time we opened fire the army spokesman announces we're being fired at".' Goodman also reported another curious interpretation of ceasefire violations:

> The Defence Minister admitted on television on Friday, 25 June, that the IDF did not always return fire at the same spot Israeli forces sustained fire. A rifle bullet loosed off by a Syrian soldier in the Bekaa could, theoretically, unleash a 16-hour bombardment of West Beirut. It is a pity that it took the Defence Minister two weeks to admit that this was the IDF's policy.

The main headline, across five columns of the front page of the *Jerusalem Post* on Tuesday 8 June, proclaimed, 'Tyre, Beaufort Fall as IDF Operation Nears Completion'. This only goes to show that even the shrewd and experienced journalists of the *Post*, with good links to the Israeli establishment, completely believed the first Cabinet announcement declaring war on 6 June.

But the 25-mile security limit that featured in that announcement was 25 miles from where? Twenty-five miles north of Ras Nakura on the coast, or 25 miles from Metulla, at the tip of Israel's 'finger' which, latitudinally, was 15 miles north of Ras Nakura? Begin used this ambiguity to deceive President Reagan. When the President, having tried and failed to stop the invasion on the morning of Sunday the 6th, asked Begin to halt the advance on the evening of Monday the 7th, because the Israeli army was 25 miles inside Lebanon, Begin answered that the front line was only 10 miles from Metulla. (According to Hirsh Goodman, *Jerusalem Post* 8 June, the basic goals of the operation were to be achieved within 48 hours; this mission was completed by mid-afternoon on Monday the 7th, 17 hours ahead of schedule, hence that optimistic *Post* headline.)

The official Opposition, the Labour Party, which supported the objective of a 25-mile security zone, spotted the expanding nature of the Begin-Sharon objectives as early as the night of Monday the 7th, when Peres and Rabin jointly expressed their doubts to Begin 'so that Israel did not bite off more than it could chew'. Begin obviously mollified them, because for the rest of the war Labour confined its opposition to well-mannered but ineffectual mumblings; ineffectual because Sharon had planned the operation months before.

On 27 May, during his visit to the US, when he informed Washington of his invasion plans, he told the *Wall Street Journal* that 'if an Israeli attack should occur, the purpose will be the destruction of the terrorist organisation and their infrastructure.' This second objective was supposed to refer to the PLO's military infrastructure in southern Lebanon. By about Thursday the 10th or Friday the 11th, the third objective had emerged, the weakening of the PLO's political infrastructure — its various headquarters in Beirut.

On Monday 13 June, Sharon informed the Knesset's Defence Committee that 'the job is done in Lebanon'. But the objectives went on expanding: now the aim, the fourth one, was the total destruction of both the political and the military infrastructure of the PLO. In pursuit of this the Israelis drew up a list of the names of 100 PLO leaders they wanted to evict from the Beirut headquarters. Finally, on 30 June, Sharon announced to the Knesset that the government had decided that 'the PLO must cease to exist'.

When the PLO showed no sign of vanishing, however, the Israelis began asking for the removal of the PLO fighters and their headquarters from Beirut; then for their removal from all of Lebanon, along with the Syrian troops in Beirut; then for the removal of all PLO personnel, military and non-military, from Lebanon; and likewise the removal of all Syrian forces from Lebanon.

By early July, Israel's political requirement was also clear: the formation of a strong unified central Lebanese government that would not only be able to prevent the PLO from using Lebanon as a base, but which would (and this was the ultimate objective) sign a peace treaty with Israel, as Egypt had done.

It is important to note here that all these expanded Israeli goals were shared, publicly, by the Reagan administration, according to statements made by Reagan himself, by Alexander Haig when Secretary of State and by White House and State Department spokesmen on several occasions. Israeli leaders complained, sometimes with surprise, sometimes with bitterness, that the Americans criticised Israel's actions when they themselves wanted to achieve the same objectives; they had a point.

Israelis are still asking themselves how an operation code-named 'Peace for Galilee' could result in their army occupying most of southern Lebanon, and their leaders committing themselves to such large political goals as the eviction of the Syrians from Lebanon and the imposition of a pro-Israeli

Lebanese government. Three theories are offered in explanation.

The first is that Sharon, and to a lesser extent Begin, ignored or tricked the Cabinet. Begin himself is reported to have complained that he was always told about what was going to happen after it had happened. There are well-authenticated leaks from anti-Sharon Cabinet Ministers of exactly how Sharon duped his Cabinet colleagues. Under a heading 'Ministers: Sharon strung us along', Asher Wallfish (*Jerusalem Post*, 13 June) revealed that, although it met once and sometimes twice a day, 'the cabinet never held a proper discussion on the objectives of the campaign.'

He quotes the Ministers at great length:

> Some of us felt that Sharon was keeping the implications to himself and his aims too, while merely asking us to approve a single chess move. Begin and Sharon would seek cabinet approval for only one move ahead. They did not explain the likely implications of the specific move for which they were seeking approval, implications likely to dictate the cabinet's decisions the day after. But as civilians we were like clay in the hands of the military men.

When Energy Minister Berman asked Sharon whether the advances of each day of fighting would have to be secured by an additional advance the next day, Sharon 'laughed as though he were a child caught red-handed raiding the larder, according to one of the people present'. Education Minister Hammer was one of the first to press Sharon to explain his tactics several moves ahead.

Because the Begin government was an uneasy coalition, its arrangements for running the war made it easy for Begin and Sharon to do what they wanted and bypass the Cabinet. Instead of handing over the conduct of the war, as in the past, to a small inner group of four or five Ministers which could have exercised tight control, responsibility was given, because of coalition exigencies, either to the Cabinet as a whole or to a large committee.

Diffused authority, however, proved to be no authority. What was worse the Cabinet drew up a policy paper laying down general guidelines for the operation. Since Sharon had a hand in its drafting, it was suitably vague and provided him with effective cover when attacked for exceeding his authority.

The second theory is that the war just happened, one thing leading to another. This was the view put forward by Eliahu Ben-Elissar, chairman of the Knesset Defence Committee, to the *Jerusalem Post* (6 July):

> It's all a question of the momentum of battle. There was such a swift advance along the coastal road by our armour that we found ourselves swept along after Damour in order to protect what we had achieved.

If true, this does not reflect much credit on the ability of the Israeli army general staff to keep control of a battle that was being fought on the very narrow front, four to five miles wide, of the coastal plain.

Finally, there is the theory put forward by Begin himself (*Jerusalem Post*, 27 July), refuting the second theory. 'Nothing happened in this war', he declared, 'that was not planned.'

Certainly a reluctant Syria was drawn into the war by deliberately provocative actions ordered by Sharon. Asher Wallfish (*Jerusalem Post*, 15 June) claimed that Sharon had always wanted to attack the Syrian missile batteries in the Bekaa but was overruled by the Cabinet, which 'from the very start said it had no interest in a clash with Syria.'

On 13 June Sharon asked the Cabinet to approve an initiated (i.e. unprovoked) attack on the Syrians, but, to his dismay, it declined. The next day the Syrians moved more missiles and reinforcements into the Bekaa, giving Sharon his pretext to attack. But, Wallfish goes on, this Syrian move 'could have been the result of provocative manoeuvring on Sharon's part. By sending IDF units in the eastern sector forward till they virtually stood eyeball-to-eyeball with the Syrian units, he made the Syrian units feel threatened. By sending other units in the central sector to overlook the Beirut-Damascus highway he made the Syrians feel nervous and menaced by encirclement.'

Since, as we have seen, Sharon admitted that the operation had been planned months ahead, Begin's boast seems the best explanation for Israel's expanded military campaign and expanded political goals: from the start Israel knew what it wanted.

Has Israel, however, achieved what it wanted? Setting aside the larger, long-term political objectives and considering only the more immediate military goals, the answer would seem to be a big no and a small yes. Yes, the PLO's military infrastructure in southern Lebanon was destroyed and the fighters and the headquarters were forced to leave Beirut. No, it was not a swift, clean, surgical operation, all over in 24, 48 or 72 hours. Instead it became a clumsy, bloody, drawn-out campaign that lasted for 67 days, the second longest of Israel's wars against the weakest of its enemies.

The battle of Beirut lasted as long as it did because the Israeli army failed to sweep into Beirut in its first northward push, due to the tenacity of the PLO and Lebanese fighters at Tyre, Sidon, Damour and Khaldeh. This dislocated the Israeli army timetable. Moreover, in the house-to-house and hand-to-hand fighting the Palestinian and Lebanese fighters inflicted such heavy casualties on the Israelis that they did not dare repeat the experience on a larger scale in Beirut. The pattern of battle in Beirut was imposed on the Israeli army by its enemy.

In the end, the 'defeated' Palestinian guerrilla was confirmed in his belief that, man to man, he was a better and braver fighter than the Israeli, who had only prevailed because of his vastly superior weaponry. This is why the fighters left Beirut with their heads held high. In *Al-Hamishmar* on 15 July P. Sever declared:

> In war there are no draws. Whoever does not win loses. We have not defeated the PLO. We have not defeated it militarily and therefore we

have lost . . . If the PLO had fled and its fighters had scattered in all directions the victory would have been ours. But the PLO fighters stayed in the city, dug in and fought.

The only alternative left to the Israeli army was the policy of 'static fire', of indiscriminate bombardment that brought down on it the outrage and condemnation of the world, even eventually of Reagan himself.

2. Fire and Sword

'O my God, make them like a wheel; as the stubble before the
   wind.
As the fire burneth a wood, and as a flame setteth the mountains
   on fire;
So persecute them with thy tempest, and make them afraid with
   thy storm . . .
Yea let them be put to shame and perish:
That men may know that thou, whose name alone is Jehovah,
   art the most high over all the earth.'

From Psalm 83, recommended for daily public reading by the Rabbinate
of Israel during time of war.

Whether or not it was in answer to the psalmist's savage supplication, the
Israeli armed forces did indeed bring down fire and flame and man-made
tempest and storm upon the battlefields of southern Lebanon — the towns
of Tyre and Sidon, Nabatieh and Damour and the Palestinian refugee camps
of Ain Helweh and Rachidieh.

   The Israelis were among the first to admit it. Abraham Rabinovich wrote
(*Jerusalem Post*, 18 June):

   Israel's incursion into Lebanon certainly was not planned by 'The
   Committee for the Improvement of Israel's Image'. The sight of the
   gutted towns of Tyre and Sidon is numbing; it would provide grist for
   propaganda-mills so long as pictures of devastated cities have impact.
   A very sketchy survey found no serious hits on mosques and churches;
   but just about every other structure had been bombed, shelled and
   machine-gunned.

   A veteran Israeli soldier, reserve Lt.-Col. Dov Yirmiya (*Al-Hamishmar*,
16 July), wrote:

   Crossing the frontier I saw the devastation along the road. The climax
   the city of Tyre . . . the commercial centre with its many shops and
   workshops is totally destroyed . . . the Palestinian hospital of the

Israeli forces enter Sidon (Al-Safir)

terrorists suffered a direct hit and part of it has collapsed. Expensive and sophisticated equipment is half buried under the ruins and the sickening stink of bodies is horrible. Among the dead we discover the body of an Israeli soldier killed three days ago.

Even though Christopher Walker of *The Times* (1 July) said that 'the awful destruction' in Tyre, which rendered it 'almost unrecognisable', was much worse than at Sidon, his colleague, Robert Fisk (*The Times*, 19 July) said:

> The Israeli air attacks [on Sidon] must have been among the most ferocious ever delivered on a Lebanese city [this was before Beirut's ordeal]. In the southern sector of Sidon it looks as if a tornado has torn through the residential buildings and blocks of flats ripping off balconies and roof supports, tearing down massive walls and collapsing whole blocks. There are still dead in these ruins too.

David Ignatius of the *Wall Street Journal* (22 June) reported that 'in the central areas of town about one in every three buildings had taken a direct hit from Israeli bombs or artillery.' For Eric Silver (*The Guardian*, 21 June), 'Sidon was a chilling sight: two out of every three buildings gape black and empty.' Yet in Sidon Israeli fire could be both indiscriminate and highly selective. Françoise Chipaux (*Le Monde*, 17 June) reported that 'the town centre is three-quarters destroyed. The only buildings spared were the churches, mosques, hospitals and administrative buildings.'

Not quite the only ones, because she also says that 'none of the buildings containing PLO arms dumps were hit during the bombardment, which leads one to believe that Israeli intelligence knew where they were'. Also 'none of the buildings along the broad boulevard along the seafront were spared, except the local office of the PLO, doubtless because of its arms depot'. This clearly indicates that when buildings were hit at random it was because the Israelis were indulging, deliberately, in random bombardment.

Joining in the controversy that soon arose over the extent of the destruction and the casualties, Benny Morris (*Jerusalem Post*, 13 July) said,

> Government and IDF statements about destruction in Sidon are absurd. Major destruction of houses fans out throughout the city and is not restricted to the two main streets, which indeed were badly mauled.

What were these 'absurd' official estimates? One official told the press that only 10 houses in Tyre had been damaged beyond repair, and even fewer in Sidon. This official propaganda was deliberately concocted back in Jerusalem, because in the *Jerusalem Post* (15 June) Major Yosef Dana, a lecturer in Arabic literature from Haifa University serving as officer in charge of civilians, said that in Tyre '30% of the structures have been totally destroyed'.

An unofficial and comprehensive survey of destruction in Tyre was soon made, and was released by 'Israeli relief workers in Jerusalem' (David Shipler of the *New York Times*, 20 June). This estimated that damage in Tyre to buildings alone could be valued at $75 million. 'The report lists 310 dwellings as destroyed and 1,550 damaged, 250 of them seriously. Three hospitals and 14 schools are listed by name as damaged.'

It took much longer for a detailed report on damage in Sidon to appear, but on 24 August Israel radio reported an official survey as estimating that it would need $100 million to repair damage because 6,000 buildings had been damaged, 1,500 of them beyond repair or 'flattened'. Major Arnon Mozer, officer in charge of civilians in Sidon, said that, apart from 5-6% of buildings destroyed and 10% 'moderately damaged, lesser damage was suffered by virtually every other structure'.

Engineers from Israel's most prestigious technical institution, the Haifa Technion, nevertheless repeated the official claim that only about 10 buildings in Tyre were damaged beyond repair. These official figures were absurd given Israeli tactics. A parachute officer declared (*Davar*, 28 June):

> Our slogan was to enter urban settlements while fighting, but to cause minimum damage to houses. When the main aim is to save our own human lives, this slogan doesn't work. In this kind of operation, with a co-ordinated action of tanks, artillery and airforce in urban areas, massive destruction of houses is unavoidable . . . The only way would have been not to enter Sidon: I assumed that was not the aim of the operation.

Equally heavy damage was inflicted on Damour and Nabatieh by the Israelis, but Damour had been fought over before so it was not possible to say how much destruction was caused by Israeli action. But at Nabatieh, 'crushed by Begin's sledgehammer' (*Financial Times*, 15 June), Stewart Dalby described a familiar scene: 'Rows of houses were missing, walls and roofs ripped off.' The Israelis had 'softened up the town before moving in'. Dalby quoted a resident, 'Oh yes, the Israelis started bombing on Saturday night, all night they bombed.'

Even at Chtaura, on the other side of the Lebanon range where there had been no nearby fighting, Patrick Cockburn (*Financial Times*, 26 June) described it as 'empty and shattered, the buildings gutted by rockets and bombs . . . the neighbouring hotels all appear to have suffered damage from shells or bombs.'

Accounts of damage inflicted or casualties caused in southern Lebanon always contain the proviso that they do not refer to the five Palestinian refugee camps in the area. As Christopher Walker reported in *The Times* as late as 9 July, a month after the hostilities began:

> For reasons of personal safety and political prudence the Israeli authorities are continuing to prohibit all reporters from entering the shell of the Ain Hilweh refugee camp in Sidon. [Walker said that he was

taken to the camp 'by mistake' and that] after spending an hour wandering along tracks recently bulldozed through 20-foot-high mounds of stinking rubble . . . the motives for the ban become easier to understand.

(Israeli army conducting officers who took foreign correspondents to these camps even by mistake were threatened with punishment.)

David Richardson, a reporter for the *Jerusalem Post* (9 July):

The bombs did not leave any craters here in Ain Hilweh . . . they appear to have exploded just above the surface, saving all the force of their blast for the thin walls of the refugee houses. Ain Hilweh now is some two square kilometres of twisted broken rubble, putrid rubbish and torn and shattered personal belongings . . . .

At first glance there are few signs of battle in the camp. It could have been struck by an earthquake or systematically razed by bulldozers . . . . It cannot be recognized now but one of the largest buildings in Ain Hilweh was the local mosque. The bulldozers that had worked their way along the road had pushed the rubble of the mosque into a slightly higher mound, but otherwise it's just another bump in the devastated landscape. 'That is the will of Allah — and of Zionism,' a student said.

Describing conditions in the other large refugee camp, Rachidieh outside Tyre, two other *Post* reporters, Morris and Bernstein, wrote (18 July):

Every third house lies in ruins, blown up by IDF sappers because it contained what one army spokesman described as 'terrorist bunkers'. Most other houses suffered from damage and cracks from detonations.

A dry, factual report on the damage in the five camps issued by the United Nations Relief and Works Agency for Palestine Refugees (UNRWA) on 23 June, stated:

Mieh Mieh camp slightly damaged. Bourj el-Shemali: 35% of refugee houses destroyed. El-Buss camp: 50% of refugee houses destroyed. UNRWA Food Distribution Centre, one school, feeding centre and handicraft centre destroyed. Rachidieh camp: 70% of refugee houses destroyed. UNRWA buildings seriously damaged. Ain Hilweh camp: totally destroyed.

Ain Hilweh, incidentally, means sweet spring. It housed 35,000 Palestinians; Rachidieh housed 15,000. Why were they destroyed? Ain Hilweh became a battleground because guerrillas there refused to surrender. The Israeli account, which is probably true, is that they held back for two days trying to talk the fighters out. Then leaflets were dropped giving civilians two hours to leave. Many did but not all.

> Then the air bombardment began. The camp was systematically reduced to rubble. Finally Israeli troops in armoured personnel carriers inched their way in behind bulldozers. Eventually all the terrorists were killed in firefights and their bunkers were dynamited.

This is Richardson's account of the battle of Ain Hilweh, which lasted for six days. After the fighting was over and the last 'terrorist' had been killed or captured, the bombing went on and on, and then the bulldozers razed whatever was left standing. Richardson, writing for an Israeli paper and mindful of the ever-watchful Israeli military censor, hinted at the truth when he wrote, 'It could have been systematically razed by bulldozers.'

Ain Helweh refugee camp, near Sidon (UNRWA)

It was. Why? Because it was Israeli policy not to allow UNRWA to reconstitute the refugee camps, for the camps are the physical, organised presence of the Palestinian people.

As to the dynamiting of one out of every three houses in Rachidieh because of the 'bunkers', even the official Israeli spokesman is reported as saying, 'One house in every three had a bunker or air-raid shelter. A camp inhabitant claimed that while some of the bunkers were used by the PLO "most were used as family air-raid shelters" ' (Morris and Bernstein, *Jerusalem Post*, 18 July).

The military spokesman in Rachidieh said, 'There was a terrorist in every house.' There probably was a fighter in every house: there could have been one in every family, just as there is in Israel during mobilisation, and there was a general mobilisation of all Palestinian males aged 16 to 24.

One Israeli, Lt.-Col. Zvi Lanir, criticised the Israeli government (*Yediot Ahronot*, 24 August), saying that the Palestinian inhabitants of the camps all belonged to the PLO because the organisation ran the camps, provided social assistance, found them jobs, etc. But the camp people were 'not terrorists' and Israelis 'had no reason to destroy the camps'.

A student in Ain Hilweh told Richardson that

> he had never felt threatened by the presence of the PLO or the existence of their headquarters and stores in the centre of the camp. 'They were here to protect me,' he explained with slight astonishment.

Yet the camps were attacked, and UNRWA estimated that in the five camps near Tyre and Sidon 50% of the refugee homes were destroyed. To this must be added the total, systematic levelling by bombardment of the three large camps near Beirut — Bourj el-Barajneh, Sabra and Chatila, housing about 80,000 people — which had been bombed many times long before the war and which bore the brunt of the battle of Beirut.

Begin produced a singularly clumsy excuse for Israel's massive destruction of Lebanese towns and Palestinian refugee camps. The West, he said, had no right to criticise Israel, because of what Germany had done to Coventry, and Britain to Dresden, in World War II. Outraged Israelis pointed out that these acts had been recognised, even by Britain and Germany, as acts of horror and terror.

The Human Cost

Even before the controversy over the degree of physical destruction in southern Lebanon broke out, a fiercer controversy erupted over the human cost to civilians. It all began on 12 June when Fracesco Noseda, head of the International Committee of the Red Cross (ICRC), declared that 'more than 600,000 people have been driven from their homes as a result of Israel's invasion of Lebanon' and that there were 10,000 dead.

The main but not the only reason for the high human cost of this war is the one already referred to — the massive use of firepower against densely populated urban areas in order to save Israeli lives. This direct testimony of one veteran Israeli soldier, fighting in his second war, was given to Daniel Gavron (*Jerusalem Post*, 9 July):

> He [the soldier] agreed that there were orders from above not to harm civilians; but claims that when you are ordered to advance, firing, into a refugee camp, these orders become meaningless, particularly after the camp had been mercilessly shelled and bombed beforehand. 'It brings home to you the problem of *toar haneshk*, the purity of arms. There was a purity of light weapons, not purity of artillery,' he says flatly. 'We made the moral calculation, our superiors did not.' Moreover the bombing had indeed been directed at PLO targets, the terrorists had been safe in their bunkers. The only casualties of the bombing have been innocent civilians, in his opinion.

How could there not be heavy civilian casualties when, for instance, as James McManus reported to *The Guardian* (8 July), 'The Israeli gunners are now firing at almost point blank range' into the suburbs of West Beirut?

The difficulty of arriving at a reasonably accurate figure for the dead, the wounded and the homeless was that one had to juggle with three sets of figures — one provided by international agencies and by foreign correspondents reporting on a single town or incident; another provided by Lebanese sources, the Red Cross and the police (and these are not always the same); and a third provided by the Israelis.

One difficulty was that the recovery and counting of the dead went on a long while after they became dead. Christopher Walker (*The Times*, 1 July) reported that, three weeks after the fighting in Tyre, there was still 'an atmosphere heavy with the unmistakeable smell of death'. Two Oxfam workers saw bodies being pulled from the rubble in Sidon on 3 July.

There is this vivid description of death in Sidon from Robert Fisk (*The Times*, 19 June):

> The young man wanted to help us; the Israelis had bombed the elementary school around the corner, he said, and there were 150 dead civilians still lying in the basement. It seemed hard to believe, but there was in the air a terrible smell . . . and through the broken roof of the basement we saw them.
>
> The bodies lay on top of each other to a depth perhaps of six feet, their arms and legs wrapped around each other, well over 100 of them, congealed in death into a strangely unnatural mass. The Red Cross now estimates that between 1,500 and 2,000 people, most of them civilians, died in this broken city and they have not had time to bury many of the dead . . . . There are other even more terrible basements around the city, and there are several mass graves where the Mayor in despair ordered the unrecognised to be placed. One such, containing 40 bodies, lies unmarked on a traffic island, half covered in garbage and rubble.

Ain Helweh refugee camp, near Sidon (UNRWA)

Ian Black (*The Guardian*, 3 July) after reporting on the 'terrible basements' of Sidon — 70 dead in one, 260 in another — concluded,

> But on the evidence gathered in Sidon, and the obvious difficulties of corroborating contradictory stories, a round sum of 3,000 dead is beginning to look a deal more accurate than figures of 10,000 and upward.

None of these figures included the dead from the Palestinian refugee camps.
Christopher Walker, reporting from Ain Hilweh, in *The Times* (9 July), said:

> There was no way of telling how many bodies still lay below the smashed buildings and twisted heaps of masonry. An Israeli lieutenant-colonel said frankly that it was impossible to estimate the figure accurately. One informed guess from local Lebanese medical sources was about 600 dead in Ain Hilweh, including both guerrillas and civilian camp dwellers.

After consulting the lists kept by one old grave digger in one cemetery in Beirut, Robert Fisk (*The Times*, 2 July) concluded:

> If just the small corner of Sabra contains 250 casualties from the last month of fighting, there must be a few thousand dead scattered across West Beirut's eight cemeteries. Hospital figures bear this out: 270 men, women and children died on just the second day of Israeli bombing in Beirut last month.

The first Lebanese figure, from the Red Cross on 13 June, was that at least 1,000 civilians had been killed and 3,000 wounded in the Israeli capture of Sidon alone. On 14 June the Lebanese police said that 9,583 people had been killed and 16,608 wounded since the start of the Israeli air raids on 4 June. On 7 July the overall officially reported casualties throughout Lebanon stood at 10,134 killed and 17,337 injured.

Yet two weeks earlier Robert Fisk (*The Times*, 21 June), by painstakingly adding up the separate figures given by the Red Cross and the Lebanese police for each town and village, reached the total of 14,000 people killed and up to 20,000 people wounded. After the first week the casualties occurred mostly in and around Beirut, and the final figure for that area up to 12 August, when at Reagan's insistence the bombardment ceased, was 5,000 killed.

Waking up after two weeks of the war to the fact that, however successful on the field of battle, Israel was losing the propaganda battle, Israel's Foreign Ministry on 22 June announced that 460 to 470 civilians had been killed and 1,600 wounded in southern Lebanon, excluding Beirut. The breakdown was 400 killed in Sidon, 50-60 in Tyre and 10 in Nabatieh. These figures excluded Palestinian casualties.

Later, without explanation, the Israeli figure was revised downwards to 265 dead in Sidon, 56 in Tyre and 10 in Nabatieh, or a total of 331 killed. An American correspondent was moved to ask Meridor, the minister in charge of relief operations in south Lebanon, whether the figure meant that he believed 'in the possibility of resurrection' (*Jerusalem Post*, 16 July). Around 5 July Meridor had said that 'the total number of Arab dead in southern Lebanon – Lebanese and Palestinian civilians and PLO – was 231'; two weeks earlier he had said that the figure was 214.

However, speaking to correspondents just outside Beirut, the Israeli army spokesman, Col. Paul Kedar, said that 'only a few thousand' Lebanese civilians had been killed. As regards the figures for Palestinians, on 7 July Meridor said that in the refugee camps outside Sidon and Tyre another 1,200 persons had died, 'combatants and non-combatants'.

There was the same confusion in Israeli figures for the number of PLO fighters killed. Three weeks earlier, on 19 June, General Eitan said that the Israeli forces had killed 'some 2,000 terrorists', while a week later, on 27 June, Major-General Yariv claimed that '1,000 terrorists' had been killed.

In trying to sift through the various estimates, and even taking into account Fisk's tabulation of 14,000 killed by 21 June, perhaps the most reasonable estimate of civilians killed in southern Lebanon and Beirut is 12,000, with a possible upper figure of 15,000 or more. At the end of August the respected independent Beirut newspaper *Al-Nahar* reported the Lebanese government casualty figures as 18,000 dead and 30,000 wounded – including the PLO and Lebanese fighters killed, who probably numbered no more than 2,000 dead in all. Thus the final figure for civilian dead would be around 16,000 which is not far off our maximum figure.

It is possible to arrive at some tolerably realistic figures for the killed because, even in wartime conditions, deaths are reported to the police or by hospitals, and the dead have to be buried. But no such tally was kept for the wounded, because the hospitals were much too busy to keep records except for the most serious cases; and many of the wounded would have been treated in private clinics or improvised first-aid stations with no records kept. But if the dead numbered between 12-15,000 the wounded could not have been less than 40,000; the official figure of 30,000 would seem to be on the low side.

When presenting their figures of casualties, the Israelis recount their story of the warning leaflet. According to this, the Israeli airforce dropped leaflets on Tyre and Sidon warning the inhabitants to leave, there was a pause for two hours, and then the bombardment began. The warning thus put the lives of Israeli soldiers at risk.

The truth of the leaflet story emerges, however, when we ask: when were the leaflets dropped – before or during the bombardment?

The aerial bombing of Tyre and Sidon did not begin following the Israeli army's crossing of the frontier on Sunday, 6 June: as at Nabatieh, it began on Saturday and went on through the night. Once the armoured forces of the Israelis crossed the frontier at about 10am on Sunday they

Ain Helweh refugee camp, near Sidon (UNRWA)

were at Tyre in a couple of hours, and the land bombardment then joined in. The land bombardment of Sidon, by tanks and artillery, began on Monday morning. Both towns had come under naval bombardment by Sunday midday.

Rachidiyeh refugee camp, near Tyre (UNRWA)

There are eyewitness accounts, from the news agencies, of events in Tyre and Sidon on Sunday, and of the flight of civilians under the bombing; there is no mention of leaflets. Instead we have one clear continuous account of what happened in Sidon between Saturday and Monday. It was given to Stewart Dalby (*Financial Times*, 17 June) by Carol Ghanloush, the British wife of a Lebanese Shia Muslim jeweller.

> The first they knew of the Israeli advance was Saturday when there was continuous bombing. When the bombing continued unbroken for 36 hours Mrs Ghanloush prepared to leave. The next day the Israelis dropped leaflets.

That was on Monday. The same thing happened at Tyre, where Christopher Walker (*The Times*, 1 July) reported that it was 'before the final assault' that the leaflets were dropped. But on Saturday night, the whole of Sunday and Sunday night the 'softening-up' bombardment went on. This timetable is confirmed by Sharon himself. Speaking to the Knesset (Israeli parliament) on 29 June 'he quoted from a senior staff discussion on Monday night, 7 June, on the need to avoid civilian casualties in Tyre and Sidon, even if this caused greater danger to the IDF'. By Monday night the war and the bombardment of Tyre and Sidon had, officially, been going on for 36 hours.

What happened to the people of Tyre and Sidon who went to the beaches as the Israeli leaflets asked them to do? At Sidon: 'The evacuation was terrible,' Mrs Ghanloush said. 'They carried the sick and wounded out of the hospitals and dumped them on the beaches. Everyone had to run for it, there was no time for anything.' The hospitals were evacuated because they had already become targets.

Yet these people were lucky compared to those on the Tyre beaches. Lt.-Col. Dov Yirmya (*Al-Hamishmar*, 16 July) wrote:

> On 10 June the commander told me to begin taking care of water supplies for about 50,000 people still concentrated at the seashore, including babies and old people from all over the town. [On the 10th the people had been on the open beach, without shelter, for 72 hours.] Apparently those who planned this operation did not even think about this possibility and did not prepare water and food for so many prisoners and for a population in such large numbers and for an indefinite period of time. [In effect everyone on the beach was a prisoner, because as soon as they had assembled the Israelis put barbed-wire fences around them and no one was allowed out until all the men had been screened.]
>
> And the cost of preparing bread and water for these people is lower than the cost of one flight by one bombarding plane. Oh yes, they prepared for the people: one truck with 1,600 loaves of bread. We also have one water tanker which is kept for our unit's needs and not for the thousands of people. Under my pressure the tanker is given to the imprisoned people. The sun is strong, the people are hysterical. Cries, shouts and begging. The water tanker is empty within half an hour. I demand at least three more water tankers. The commander promises. All in the same calm, indifferent manner.

Fortunately help was given by other soldiers. Moved by their sufferings the soldiers of a neaby Unifil unit tried to take them food and water. They were physically prevented by the Israelis. On a second attempt the UN men, by now angry, pushed the Israelis aside and crossed the barbed wire. Later, on 4 August, Israeli tanks tried to move into West Beirut and loudspeaker trucks urged the population to make for the beaches. The story of the Tyre beaches had spread. The Beirutis stayed put and the tanks were beaten back.

The ICRC rapidly scaled down its initial figure of 600,000 homeless to half that number, and this may be accepted, but again as a minimal figure. The number of Palestinian homeless can be fixed accurately, because of UNRWA records: 47,000 in the south and 76,000 around Beirut; 123,000 in all. This figure is for refugees registered with UNRWA; but there are also unregistered refugees who were also rendered homeless. Since there were many more Lebanese than Palestinians living in the south, though Lebanese civilian areas were not demolished like some of the camps, there must have been at least as many Lebanese homeless.

With the attention of the media focused on events in southern Lebanon and Beirut not much attention was given to the effects of the war on the people of the Bekaa Valley, even though the battles between the Syrians and the Israelis in the southern valley brought death and destruction upon civilians there too. In fact, the northern area of the Bekaa, especially Baalbek, received refugees not only from other parts of the valley but from Beirut and even from southern Lebanon. On 23 July Michael Simmons (*The Guardian*) reported that 70,000 homeless people had crammed into Baalbek's schools and public buildings; Marvine Howe (*New York Times*, 19 July) quotes a figure of 100,000. The Israeli figure for the homeless in southern Lebanon was 20,000 persons.

Even among the homeless some were more fortunate than others. The more fortunate were those that had some sort of roof over their heads – in half-built or abandoned buildings, schools, cinemas, the hallways or base-ments of apartment blocks. The less fortunate were those without a roof, who had camped out in olive groves or citrus orchards or, as in Beirut, in public parks. We have a figure for the shelterless in south Lebanon. The British relief organisation Oxfam estimated that on 12 August they numbered 100,000.

Then there were the destitute: the people who had lost their source of income. Most of these were included among the homeless and shelterless, but there were many Lebanese and Palestinians who had not suffered injury, and were still in their own homes, but had no work or income because their shops, workshops, offices or factories had been destroyed, or whose type of work was not wanted.

A spokesman for Unicef, in a statement on 30 June, said that 'more than 900,000 mothers and children have been left destitute without homes or incomes . . . this was a conservative estimate, but was more reliable than previous reports made in the heat of battle'. Subtracting the homeless from that large figure still leaves hundreds of thousands without income .

Depopulation and Dispersal

This was the policy deliberately applied by Israel against the population of the refugee camps in southern Lebanon. The camp population numbered about 60,000 in all and the Israelis did not want them to go on living in the camps. This is why Ain Hilweh was bombed for days after the fighting stopped, and was then bulldozed.

This is why, according to Col. Yirmiya, the Rachidieh camp 'was being destroyed two weeks after all its inhabitants had fled so that it shall never

again give shelter to them'. The colonel recorded that when, on 18 June,
Meridor visited Sidon and was asked,

> What is the policy regarding the Palestinian refugees, he replies, 'They
> should be driven eastward' — waving his arms in the direction of Syria
> — 'Let them go there and don't let them return'.

The Israelis even tried to stop them returning to the bulldozed camps,
as witnessed by Everett Mendelsohn, head of a Quaker mission of inquiry
(Reuters, 5 August):

> There are now 6,000 to 10,000 people out there on the rubble, with
> the Israelis refusing to let them pitch tents. They are also refusing to
> allow water pipes or a sewer system to be rebuilt there.

Col. Yirmiya again: 'The prohibition which was inflicted on them to put
up tents, which are in good supply in the UNRWA stores, is an inhuman and
wicked act.' Meridor, according to Reuters' correspondent in Tel-Aviv, Arik
Bachar, 'does not want the refugees to return to camps south of Sidon.' (All
of UNRWA's five camps are south of Sidon.)

In mid-August the sheer pressure of circumstances forced the Israelis
to permit UNRWA to give the refugees tents and to let them pitch them near
the ruins of the old camps. But this was seen only as a temporary stage. The
long-term Israeli aim, according to 'a senior Israeli government official',
(*Jerusalem Post*, 3 August) was to shut down the camps and 'end the anti-
Israeli hatred they had bred by housing the refugees in new buildings dispersed in various parts of the major cities of Tyre, Sidon and Nabatieh'.

While Israel laid down these prohibitions and drew up its ambitious
plans for dispersal 'the official clearly implied that Israel would not
contribute funds to either stage of the resettlement. That will be left to the
Lebanese because we recognise Lebanese sovereignty over the area.' In
addition to Lebanon, the official said, perhaps the United States or the
Arab countries would pay to implement Israel's plans for dispersing the
Palestinian refugees.

The Terror Weapons

If, according to the Israelis, the use of leaflets supposedly decreased the
number of civilian casualties, their use of new terror weapons undoubtedly
increased that number. Those used extensively were air-burst bombs, fragmen-
tation bombs and shells, cluster bombs, phosphorus bombs and shells, and
possibly a new 'vacuum' bomb.

As to their overall effect on casualty figures, David Ottaway (*The Guardian*,
18 June) quoted Dr Abu Walid, chief surgeon of a hospital in Beirut's Sabra
refugee camp:

The rate of mortality among victims brought in for operation was very high. He said that during the 1978 invasion it had been 15% to 20%, but that this time it was between 30% and 50%. He attributed the higher rate to the kind of weapons being used by the Israelis.

David Hirst (*The Guardian*, 8 July) quoted another doctor as saying that the ratio of dead to wounded, instead of being the usual one to five, was about one to one.

The use of phosphorus shells was signalled from the very first day of the war. David Shipler (*New York Times*, 10 June) reported that

> the United Nations command of Unifil was understood to have protested to Israel over the use of incendiary artillery shells in the attack on Tyre on Sunday. An Israeli army spokesman denied that such shells had been used.

The UN officer conceded that white phosphorus shells were not banned by the Geneva Convention but were infrequently used because they were considered extremely harmful. They continued to be used sporadically by the Israelis during June and July.

It was in August, during the heavy bombardment of West Beirut, that ample and conclusive evidence became available of the extensive use of phosphorus shells, and this was reported by many correspondents. Loren Jenkins (*Washington Post*, 21 August) reported that

> dozens of 155mm shells dug from the rubble have hollowed interiors coated with yellowish-orange oxide and the pungent odour of phosphorus is unmistakable. Other phosphorus shells have hit the city's centre in the vicinity of the Hamra street business district. At least two of the city's 19 hospitals have reported being hit by the shells.

The Times (2 July) reported:

> Several hundred phosphorus shells have been fired into Beirut by the Israelis over the past two weeks. Ironically, one of them hit the roof of a local Red Cross Office distinguished by the large white smoke cloud emitted from their explosion.

This office was also distinguished by several large Red Cross flags flying from its roof: the shell impacted between two of the flags.

The Times explained:

> Phosphorus bombs and shells are regarded as routine ammunition in most western armies which use the projectiles as artillery markers or smoke screens. However, their use is generally confined to open battlefields, and three protocols agreed at a 1980 United Nations

convention in Geneva contain broad restrictions on the use of incendiary weapons against military objectives located in residential areas of towns and cities . . . Israel was herself represented at this conference.

Thus Israel used these shells freely in the precise circumstances in which they were restricted by the three protocols of the 1980 UN Convention. Both Robert Fisk and Loren Jenkins gave grim accounts of the effect of the shells. Fisk:

> Dr Shamaa found that two five-day-old twins had already died. But they were still on fire. 'I had to take the babies and put them in buckets of water to put out the flames,' she said. 'When I took them out half an hour later they were still burning. Even in the mortuary they smouldered for hours'.

Jenkins:

> Troy Rusli, a Norwegian doctor who is a volunteer surgeon at the make-shift Lahout Hospital at West Beirut's Near East Theological Centre, described a man, about 60, who was brought in with a piece of phosphorus-coated shrapnel lodged in his chest. 'Smoke from the burning phosphorus inside him was coming out of his nose and mouth with every painful breath,' Dr Rusli said. 'We had to cut the shrapnel out of him before we could finally stop the burning by cutting away the scorched tissues'.

'No weapon is a good weapon,' said John Barton, an American professor of medicine, also working as a volunteer. 'But this one, the phosphorus bomb, is one of the worst.'

In defence the Israelis first said that they were using the shells as artillery markers; then came the argument that, after all, others had used them in this way since World War II and, finally, that the PLO was really to blame for making their stand in civilian-occupied areas.

Correspondents in Lebanon expended considerable time and energy tracking down Israeli use of the cluster bomb, not only because it was an unusually horrible weapon, but also because its use by Israel was severely restricted by agreements with the United States, its supplier. The cluster bomb is a canister which on impact sprays up to 650 separate bomblets or grenades that then explode on impact. As *Time* magazine (12 July) put it: 'Because the bombs indiscriminately blast an area several hundred feet in diameter they are clearly unsuited for use in civilian neighbourhoods.'

The first reported Israeli use of the bomb came in the first week of the war during the battle for Ain Dara in the Chouf area, against the Syrians. David Ottaway (*Washington Post*, 19 July) reported that his colleague Jonathan Randall 'visited an Armenian sanatorium near Ain Dara that was hit by a cluster-bomb'. (This must have happened on Friday, 11 June.) In the succeeding weeks the plastic canisters of these bombs were found in several areas of Beirut; some were unexploded and were found to contain a

Cluster bomb canisters (Al-Safir)

complex electronic device for radar guidance or timing. The American manu-
facturers' code number was reported.

Faced with this accumulating and irrefutable evidence Israel broke silence
and admitted using this weapon, but in a curious way: on 26 June General
Eitan, in a letter to Israeli troops broadcast by Israeli armed forces radio,
said that eight Israeli soldiers had been injured picking up cluster-bomb
pieces in Lebanon. Finally, the next day, General Yariv came clean and
admitted that Israel had used the cluster-bomb.

This raised the question whether Israel had violated the agreements with
the US on its use. There are three such agreements, the latest dating from
1978 when the bombs were used in the Litani operation, and 'each one more
tightly worded by the United States than the previous one'. According to

Charles Mohr (*New York Times*, 1 July), Israel agreed in 1978 not to use them except in combat with 'two or more Arab states' and then 'only for defensive purposes'. In justification Israel said that Syria, an Arab state, was involved in the fighting.

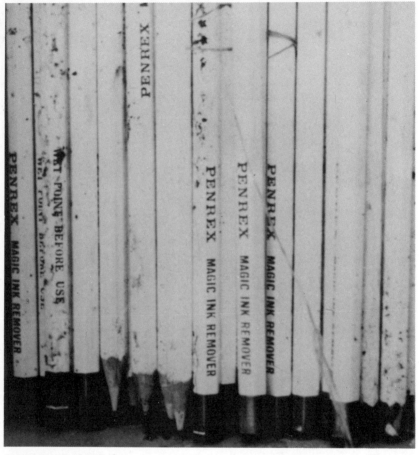

Pencil bombs (Al-Safir)

But which was the second Arab state? The PLO? As *Time* put it, 'Israel not only does not consider the PLO to be a state; it does not recognise the organisation as a legal entity.' So that US restriction on the use of the bomb was clearly violated.

As to its alleged use against military targets only, CBS News on 16 July reported CIA officials as saying they had evidence that Israel did indeed use cluster-bombs 'indiscriminately against civilian targets'. Moreover an American commission of inquiry, consisting of past and present congressional staff members, concluded that as late as 4 August cluster and phosphorus bombs were used 'indiscriminately against the civilian population of West Beirut in a minimum of 14 locations'.

As to them being used 'defensively', the Chairman of the US House Foreign Affairs Committee, Zablocki, said 'I can't by any stretch of the imagination see how using planes, tanks and artillery deep in the territory of another country is defensive' (*Jerusalem Post*, 18 July).

Israel took a month to give an explanation of its violations; thereafter the US administration would go no further in condemnation than to say that 'a substantial violation by Israel may have occurred'. As a sign of its disapproval, further shipment of 4,000 cluster-bomb shells was blocked by President Reagan. The original consignment, made in the early 1970s, was for 22,000 bombs.

One Israeli described how terrible this weapon was. The reaction of a young artillery officer, whose battery was eight kilometres south of Beirut, was described by Uri Pas (*Al-Hamishmar*, 19 July):

> The order comes in 'three cluster-bombs on target' — to support an infantry unit. The cannons operated like automatics. Every split-second delay means losses to our forces. Within a few minutes the enemy fire is silenced. The officer says, regretfully, 'If only we had this bomb during the 1973 war, it would have saved many of our soldiers'.

He also describes its destructive effect:

> The experts admit this bomb is made by Satan. The area of killing of the bomb is very large. No less is its wounding area. Watching it in operation is like watching a rain of terror. Small fatal grenades that create a horrific mushroom of death.

Mystery still surrounds the 'vacuum bombs' that implode rather than explode, causing whole buildings to collapse inwards: two bombs collapsed two tall buildings in Beirut burying 80 people in one, 120 in the other.

Why did Israel have to use these horrific weapons against the besieged city of Beirut? It had total control of the air, total control of the sea and overwhelming superiority in numbers and firepower on land.

One reason, perhaps, can be found in a Reuters report from Washington of 22 July: 'A cluster artillery shell is considered about six times as effective as a conventional artillery shell.' So can it be that the explanation is that given by General Eitan for starting the war, that if one has an effective, expensive machine to hand, one uses it, simply because it is there?

Obstructing Relief Work

On Sunday, 20 June, the *Sunday Times* of London declared in an editorial:

There is only one thing about the war in Lebanon that is beyond all dispute. Hundreds of thousands of ordinary people are on the move, needing urgent help and Israel is putting politics before their plight. It is refusing to allow UN agencies to use the food, medicines and disaster experts that have rushed to the borders of Lebanon . . . . It is not enough for Israel to say that it is coping with the situation. There is no excuse for its refusal to allow international bodies to perform their traditional roles. It is utterly appalling that the Israeli victors should obstruct these humanitarian non-political operations.

On that same day the UN Security Council, faced with Israel's two-week refusal, but unable to name it because of US objections, passed a resolution unanimously calling on 'all the parties' to allow the dispatch and distribution of aid.

The political motive referred to by the *Sunday Times* was that Israel wanted to impress on the population of southern Lebanon that, from then on, they would have to depend on Israel alone for any aid and succour. Alternatively, as suggested by a Jewish correspondent of a Swedish newspaper (*The Times*, 18 June) the Israelis were anxious to improve their international image in the wake of the invasion by being seen to provide the bulk of the aid themselves. So requests for permission to take in aid for half a dozen agencies were either refused or met with blank silence.

It has not been easy to obtain details of Israeli obstruction because aid officials are chary to talk, especially the strictly neutral International Red Cross, since they know that complaints would only make it more difficult to work with Israel in the future. But dates speak for themselves.

Within 48 hours of the Israeli attack, UNRWA, with its special responsibility for the Palestine refugees, asked for permission to send in trucks with basic food and relief supplies that were ready and waiting in Jerusalem and Gaza. But Israel has never liked UNRWA, since its programme has enabled the Palestine refugees not only to survive but to remain in being as an entity, and one that is healthy and well educated thanks to UNRWA's clinics and excellent school system.

So when, a fortnight after the war began, under international pressure, Israel gave permission for agencies to operate on 21 June, UNRWA was not included and had to wait another 24 hours for permission. That Israel yielded only under pressure was indicated by the fact that on 18 June Israel was claiming that it had received no application for aid work from Oxfam or the Save the Children Fund, which was untrue.

On 19 June the Israelis refused permission for a ship chartered by the ICRC, carrying 550 tonnes of supplies, to enter Sidon port, allegedly because it had been mined (presumably by the PLO, but the PLO did not possess marine mines). It had taken the ICRC four days to get permission for this ship to sail from Cyprus, but the Israelis do not like the Red Cross either.

Angered by the high figures for the homeless and killed put out by the

Red Cross, the Israeli Health Minister, Shostak, was indiscreet enough to say, as reported by Aryeh Rubinstein (*Jerusalem Post*, 23 June), that the Red Cross had never recognised *Magen David Adom* (the Red Star of David), or its red star symbol, in the same way that it recognised the Red Crescent of the Muslim states. 'We have a long account with the ICRC,' Shostak said. 'Its attitude towards Israel and Magen David Adom has been one of patent discrimination down the years, and we shall settle the account in the near future.'

Israel's permission to the ICRC to operate was made de facto and not de jure. The Red Cross ship arrived in Haifa on 24 June, five days later. Colonel Yermiya, who was in Sidon at the time, actually received immediate permission from Minister Meridor for this Red Cross ship to come to Sidon, but was later overruled by an army general; he made no mention of Sidon port being mined (*Al-Hamishmar*, 16 July).

As late as 23 June a Unicef relief plane was turned away from Tel-Aviv airport because, it was said, the roads into Lebanon were clogged. It had to go to Damascus, and the supplies entered over narrower and more heavily clogged roads and so reached Beirut only on 28 June.

Another way in which Israel hindered and delayed relief operations was by removing foreign doctors from local hospitals, alleging that they were 'terrorists'. Three doctors manning a mobile clinic of the Knights of Malta were expelled, and in Sidon a Canadian and two Norwegian doctors were arrested. Only after vigorous protests by their ambassadors in Israel were they released. With medical treatment desperately needed the Israeli army administration shut down the Palestinian Red Crescent Hospital in Sidon, which had a staff of 50.

No sooner had the international relief agencies started work than the Israeli authorities began to say there was too much aid (*Jerusalem Post*, 23 June). This attitude continued. On 4 July the *Observer* reported from Geneva that officials of Unicef, the UN Disaster Relief Organisation and the ICRC 'insist that Israeli authorities continue to obstruct deliveries of medicines, tents, clothes, food and water' to the displaced in southern Lebanon. Another report (*The Guardian*, 6 July) said that 'a World Council of Churches team just returned from Lebanon said the Israeli authorities were creating delays in the shipping, documentation, unloading and dis-tribution of relief and were infringing the spirit of Geneva conventions.'

When UNRWA started work the Israeli government stated that Israeli aid would go only to the Lebanese, because the Palestinians now had UNRWA to take care of them: after protests inside Israel this policy was changed, but the spirit behind it remained. UNRWA, by far the most important of the relief organisations, continued to receive only the most reluctant co-operation from the Israelis.

This attitude was of major significance for the future because, as Olof Rydbeck, the commissioner general of UNRWA, said on 20 August, it looked as if 32 years of work in UNRWA 'had been wiped out'. Israeli bombardment had left 'practically all the schools, clinics and installations of the Agency in ruins' (*New York Times*, 20 August). They would have to be rebuilt, but doing so would be immeasurably more difficult if Israel opposed it, as it was showing signs of doing.

Israel withdrew its opposition to the international agencies' relief work only when it became clear that its own relief programme was hopelessly inadequate and inappropriate. A small country like Israel simply did not have the resources to tackle a task of such magnitude, and certainly not in the middle of a war. Whatever the political motivations of Israel's leadership on the relief issue, Israel's voluntary agencies did do their best to help. But from sheer lack of experience some of this help was misguided.

As one UN official told Christopher Walker (*The Times*, 18 June):

> The Israelis are sending in completely unsuitable supplies, such as sweets and ice cream, but we are not allowed to send our regular basic rations across the border to refugees we look after.

The sweets, much-publicised, were the idea of Abie Nathan, a good-hearted but naive peacenik of Indian origin.

Unable to help the wounded, the homeless, the destitute, whose sufferings it had created, the Israeli government, as we have seen, tried to obstruct and delay the efforts of others to give them help. Of all the things Israel did in Lebanon this was the worst, for it displayed a cruelty that was calculated and callous.

We can now make a tally of the human cost of the Israeli invasion:

> 12,000 killed
> 40,000 wounded
> 300,000 homeless
> 100,000 without shelter
> and several hundreds of thousands destitute.

3. The Battle of Beirut

Speaking on television after Israel's bombing of the Fakhani quarter of Beirut in July 1981 which killed 350 civilians, Mordecai Zipori, then deputy defence minister, warned, 'If the message we sent them is insufficient, we shall send them another message.' Thus did the Begin government declare itself 'free of the restraint Israel [had] observed for decades not to bomb Beirut, and its warning that if civilians happen to be in the way, too bad'.
Douglas Watson, the *Baltimore Sun*, 22 July 1981

The southern suburbs of Beirut were bombed by Israeli warplanes on 4 June and again on the 5th. Until the armoured invasion began on the 6th Beirutis saw them as the usual 'retaliatory raids' made by Israel for attacks on Israelis. When the Israelis entered southern Lebanon on the 6th, the people of Beirut speculated on how far north they would come. They did not have long to wait.

On the night of 9 June the Israeli navy attempted to land commandos at Khaldeh beach, just 10 kilometres from the city centre. They were repulsed by Syrian tanks and Shiite militiamen belonging to the Amal group.

What are they going to do? Will they invest the city? [asked Lucien George in *Le Monde* on the 11th]. On Wednesday [9th], a candlelit night of mortal suspense, Beirutis spoke only of this. The rationed electricity, the short supply of water mattered less to them. Accustomed to much greater hardships by seven years of intermittent war, they believe they have seen everything.

But they had not. Early on the morning of the 10th, Israeli aircraft began constant overflights, dropping the first of many threatening leaflets onto the city.

This text was meant for the commander of the Syrian forces in the city:

I address this appeal to you, from one military commander to another:
The Israeli Defence Forces have been forced to enter Lebanon in order

to expel all . . . irregular factions . . . . The Israeli Defence Forces have large forces from the navy, army and airforce committed to Beirut city area, including a huge number of tanks. These forces outnumber your forces. In a short time, we will *capture the city* . . . . We therefore issued orders to our forces to permit you and your troops to leave the city without hindrance . . . . (quoted in the *Financial Times*, 11 June).

The Syrian commander in Beirut ignored the ultimatum and Israel launched heavy aerial bombardments once again on the southern suburbs of Khaldeh, the Palestinian refugee camps of Sabra, Shatilla and Bourj al-Barajneh, and the international airport and devastated the sports stadium. The Palestine News Agency claimed that 250 people had been killed and 900 wounded.

On Friday the 11th Israel entered into a ceasefire with Syria, but not with the Palestinians:

A few minutes before the mid-day ceasefire, during the heaviest bombing raid on Beirut since the invasion began six days ago, Israeli jets pounded a Palestinian neighbourhood in the southern suburbs, bringing down a six-storey building (reportedly housing al-Fatah headquarters) and damaging dozens of others . . . . During the raid, Israeli gunboats inexplicably shelled civilian areas of Muslim Beirut bringing terror to the shopping area . . . . (Eric Silver and James McManus in *The Guardian*, 12 June.)

On Saturday the 12th a ceasefire was arranged between PLO and Israeli forces for 9pm. It was the first of many of Israel's unilateral tactical ceasefires, during which Israeli forces attempted to improve their position or regroup for a new push. This was one of the second variety. Nine hours later the Israelis broke it:

As Israeli gunboats bombarded the mainland and F15 and F16 jets resumed their raids over Palestinian camps near Beirut, Israeli armoured columns successfully challenged PLO guerrillas and Lebanese Muslim militias for control of an important road junction at Khaldeh, six miles south of the capital's international airport. An Israeli convoy then rolled north-east through twisting mountain passages towards the strategic Beirut-Damascus highway.

Within hours dozens of Israeli tanks and armoured personnel carriers were parked a few hundred yards from the Presidential Palace in Baabda, five miles south-east of Beirut (*Time*, 28 June).

This was so because, after the engagement at Khaldeh, the Israelis had to do very little fighting to 'capture the city'. They simply drove their tank columns up the roads from the coast to the mountain ridge, then northwards along the ridge from the Kabr Chamoun junction to the town of Aley on the Damascus highway. En route they encountered a number of Syrian tanks, neither withdrawn nor given fighting orders by Damascus, most of which were destroyed by shelling and bombardment that also heavily damaged the villages along the road. The encirclement of West Beirut fixed the front line for seven weeks during which Israeli troops skirmished along the line with Palestinian fighters and waited to take the city by siege rather than storm.

4 June: The bombardment of Beirut which ushered in the war (AP)

But after seven weeks Defence Minister Sharon grew impatient. In the early hours of 4 August the siege was complemented with a bout of fighting – widely rumoured at the time to be the threatened major thrust. But Hirsh Goodman, the *Jerusalem Post's* defence correspondent, knew better: Israeli groups 'pushed a little deeper into the area of West Beirut under PLO control, moving about 1.2 kilometres north and taking the strategically placed Museum Hill in the north-eastern corner of the city' (5th August).

In addition, the *International Herald Tribune* (IHT) reported that 'Israeli tanks and armoured personnel carriers moved into the port at the northern end of the green line' and Israeli 'forces advanced into the Ouzai area, three miles south of the city, on the road to the airport', from where the Israeli military command claimed the force 'wiped out two PLO positions in the Bourj Barajneh refugee camp to the west, from which the guerrillas had been firing on Israeli troops' (5 August).

Goodman described the advance as one 'made by infantry, backed by artillery and tanks, and by pin-point shelling from the sea against PLO targets along the coastal road in Uzai (Ouzai).' But the shelling was clearly not confined to such targets, for the IHT reported that 'Israeli guns were firing heavily into the crowded civilian district around Hamra Street, the commercial heart of the Moslem sector,' one shell slamming into 'the Commodore Hotel, headquarters of about 200 foreign journalists' and 'the United Press International bureau . . . was hit by shellfire from Israeli gunboats' (5 August). 'Lebanon's internal security forces said at least 250 persons had been killed and 670 wounded in the Israeli attack on West Beirut on Wednesday. Many of the injured were expected to die from burns from phosphorus bombs, doctors said' (IHT, 6 August).

'The shell storm ended in a peculiarly appropriate way, with a rain of golden flares that dropped down from the clouds like the closing moments of some Wagnerian epic,' Robert Fisk wrote in *The Times* (6 August). The comparison was apt. Not only did the episode result in 'the highest casualty toll their army has suffered in any one day since the invasion' — '19 killed and 91 wounded' — but also, Fisk went on, 'such benefit as the Israelis might have gained from their assault was largely thrown away yesterday morning [5 August] when their tanks were withdrawn from their newly-won positions west of the museum and from the western end of the port . . . leaving the armour more or less where it was two days ago.' They withdrew because these 'newly-won' positions were too exposed.

All that happened to Beirut and its population between these two bouts of fighting — the only two major engagements in the battle of Beirut — was part and parcel of Israel's siege strategy aimed at driving the PLO from the city without resorting to combat in the streets, which would have cost Israel too many casualties. Thus, the Israeli Defence Forces invested the city, they bombed and shelled it, they starved its inhabitants and deprived them of water, electricity, fuel and medicines.

Siege

'We don't intend to go into Beirut,' Israeli Prime Minister Menachem Begin said in an interview with *Wall Street Journal* staff reporters David Ignatius, Frederick Kempe and Seth Lipsky on 9 July. 'But,' he adds, there are "many other ways" of forcing the PLO out.'

The way Israel chose was an old-fashioned three-pronged siege strategy involving bombardment, blockade and psychological pressure. But the siege was unique because, although all these punishments were indeed inflicted on Beirut and its population, the real target of the siege was the Reagan administration in Washington, 7,000 miles away.

It was an ingenious adaptation of a classical military strategy — and it worked because Israel did achieve the withdrawal of PLO forces from Beirut without making any major concessions, such as the pull-back of Israeli

Abu Shaker Street, Beirut (Al-Safir)

forces demanded by both the Lebanese and the Palestinians at the beginning of the negotiations in late June and early July. From that moment until the 11th ceasefire on 12 August, when the negotiations were nearly completed, Israel imposed its will on Beirut, the PLO and the Americans by bombing, starving and terrorising the city. Thus Washington was compelled to give Israel in the negotiations what Israel was not prepared to fight for in the streets of Beirut.

But was the evacuation of Beirut by the PLO worth winning at the price of what Robert Fisk — just 10 days into the invasion Israel called its 'war against terrorism' — described as 'terrorising the entire civilian population of West Beirut and killing hundreds of people' (*The Times*, 15 June)?

Although the PLO was the declared target of the siege strategy and a number of its fighters were killed and its installations destroyed in the bombardments, the strategy did not directly secure the PLO evacuation.

The bombardments did not do the trick, not even during the stepped-up raids and shelling which began on 1 August and ended on the 12th after an uninterrupted 11 hours of pounding. On 17 August John Kifner wrote, in the IHT, that the bombardments had

> had little effect on the Palestinian guerrillas in and around West Beirut . . . . While large sections of the city . . . have been pounded into rubble, the guerrillas are emerging from basement shelters, holes and sand-bagged positions almost unscathed . . . where the guerrillas have lost men, it has been mainly in fixed, exposed positions . . . Doctors at hospitals and first-aid centres say the overwhelming majority of victims are civilians.

Nor did the blockade. After nearly a month of its imposition, Thomas L. Friedman wrote:

> The Israeli blockade has yet to have any effect on the guerrillas. While visiting Position 1 (in the Ouzai area) a truck drove up dropping off piles of freshly baked loaves of Arabic bread, fresh figs, water and tinned meats and fish. The guerrillas said they have enough canned food and rice to last for six months and insisted that a visitor take some figs back with him to West Beirut (IHT, 31 July-1 August).

Nor did the psychological warfare. On 13 July David Hirst of *The Guardian* wrote of the high morale of Palestinian fighters in one of the most exposed and heavily attacked positions, at Tahwita near the international airport.

> Unlike in the city proper, the Palestinians have built no artificial defences here. Lush vegetation provides all the cover they need. There was an Israeli position just 200 yards away. 'Just think of it as 600 feet . . . . It sounds safer,' said Youssef, a volunteer from the Palestinian

diaspora who had returned to Beirut from a comfortable job in Phoenix, Arizona. The picture the guerrillas convey (of the IDF) is that of a great military machine hamstrung by fear of high casualties, and reliance on high technology.

The commander, Abu Khalid, and his men, said Hirst, 'have no illusions like anybody else, about Israel's ability to defeat them by destroying Beirut.'

In the end, as the destruction of Beirut came near, they had to go on Israel's terms. It was explained in an editorial published on 8 August in the PLO's newspaper *Filistin al-Thawra*: 'We have taken a decision for military withdrawal from Beirut because the destruction of Beirut over the heads of half a million Muslims is not a mere possibility but has become a reality.' The editorial should have said 'total and unconditional withdrawal' because the PLO had accepted that its military wing and leadership would have to leave during the third week of June.

Political Bombardment

'We will not reply . . . in words. Our reply shall be couched in terms of lead . . . . In roar of shell and shrapnel and in whine of machine guns will our answer be couched.'
(Jack London in *The Iron Heel*)

'The Israeli government announced that the bombardment was "local . . . limited and not political", ' Robert Fisk wrote in *The Times* after an episode he called 'the heaviest air and artillery assault on any Arab capital in recent history' (2 August). Yet there was worse to come. The bombardments which ended in the ninth ceasefire on 1 August were general, widespread and most definitely political. Furthermore, that episode was a step in the escalation — of increasingly frequent attacks, of maximum saturation over the maximum area of West Beirut. As with all the previous escalations of the bombardment of the city — and there were at least a dozen in the seven weeks since the bombing had begun on 4 June — the Israelis expected political, not military, dividends from their investment of fire and steel.

The main dividend the Israelis had in mind was total compliance with their demand for the unconditional withdrawal of PLO forces from Beirut. Whenever it looked as though they might get less than that, the Israeli armed forces stepped up the siege of the city, primarily by bombardment, which was the most spectacular way of exerting pressure. Just three weeks into the war Eric Silver and Jane Rosen wrote (in *The Guardian*, 26 June): 'Israel is now going all out to bludgeon the Palestinian guerrillas into submission.' The United Nations Security Council and General Assembly 'bent their efforts yesterday (25 June) to saving Beirut and bringing about a ceasefire in Lebanon. But no one was optimistic about the prospects.'

45

Sharon had said in a radio interview that the PLO 'was on its way to complete destruction . . . provided that Israel did not leave it alone.' He stated bluntly, 'We should not be affected by any political provocations, internal or external, that may threaten our military and political achievements;' that is, criticism of Israel's actions, and pressure to make peace. 'According to a Lebanese politician who saw . . . Mr Habib, Israel was rejecting all peace proposals. He quoted him as saying: Sharon rejects, Sharon rejects.'

On 23 June the PLO agreed in principle to withdraw from the city; on 2 July the PLO gave a formal written statement to Lebanese Prime Minister Chafiq Wazzan (*The Guardian*, 3 July). On 4 and 5 July the Israelis significantly stepped up their bombardment. Sunday the 11th was one of their record days for shelling, which 'was so intense that negotiators were unable to travel to meetings' where they were due to discuss 'the Arafat plan for a military disengagement' (IHT, 12 July). That plan included too many elements Israel did not like.

'Less than two days after President Reagan began examining a new initiative to resolve the conflict in Lebanon . . . Israeli jets swept over Beirut . . . ,' Robert Fisk wrote on 23 July (*The Times*). The new initiative, presented on 20 July, was a deal by which the US would recognise the PLO in return for PLO acceptance of UN resolutions 242 and 338, signifying the PLO's effective recognition of Israel. Fisk summed it up:

> If Israel wanted to bring these latest discussions to a sudden end, thereby preventing any chance of the PLO gaining American recognition, she could hardly have chosen a more effective method of doing so.

The Lebanese police said at least 52 people were killed or wounded in the bombing sorties (IHT, 24-25 July).

Then on Friday, 30 July

> Israeli bombardments ended the seventh ceasefire of the 55-day Lebanon crisis just as Lebanese negotiators said they had obtained an agreement in principle (once again) on a PLO withdrawal within three weeks . . . . Former Premier Saeb Salam, who has served as chief intermediary between the US special envoy and the PLO, said the agreement involved a limited Israeli withdrawal around Beirut and the deployment of a multinational force before the PLO pullout (IHT, 31 July-1 August).

Israel would accept neither of these conditions.

With Israel's point made, and taken, the negotiations went on into the first week of August. From Jerusalem, Christopher Walker reported 'a new mood of "cautious optimism" that diplomatic efforts might succeed'. An Israeli official even conceded that 'a solution might be close' (*The Times*, 9 August). On the 8th Sharon arrived in Beirut to 'hear from Mr Philip Habib . . . the

The rush to save an injured child (AP)

final plan for a Palestinian evacuation and for the arrival of a Franco-American disengagement force,' Robert Fisk reported (*The Times*, 9 August).

On the 9th: 'While the Palestine Liberation Organisation was drawing up detailed plans for the embarkation of thousands of its guerrillas from West Beirut . . . the Israelis launched a seven-hour artillery and air bombardment' (Fisk, *The Times*, 10 August). Israel wanted Habib to speed up the negotiations with the Arab countries which had agreed to accept the PLO. And on the 10th, 'shortly *after* Menachem Begin's government approved "in principle" US plans to evacuate' the PLO, Israeli planes bombed West Beirut: 'Israel . . . demanded changes in the proposal' (IHT, 11 August).

Then, on the 12th, Israel made 'its most intensive airstrikes on West Beirut since its invasion began' (IHT, 13 August). Why, when the final agreement was so near? One explanation was that the Israelis had 'objected to two elements of Mr Habib's PLO evacuation plan: the proposed participation of United Nations observers and the timing of the deployment of the peacekeeping force.' Minor points, it would seem, to cause Israel to make such an unrestrained assault on civilians, killing at least 156 and wounding 417 (IHT, 14 August).

The Lebanese Prime Minister said the PLO and Lebanese government had offered 'all the concessions requested from us and we had even reached the stage of defining the PLO's departure routes' (IHT, 13 August). One explanation was offered in a *New York Times* editorial (published in the IHT, 14-15 August): 'Those airstrikes . . . seemed calculated to disrupt, just at the point of success, the intricate peace negotiations . . . .' The editorial said that Ariel Sharon was responsible and stood accused by 'a near-unanimous Israeli Cabinet . . . of sabotaging the peace effort in Lebanon'.

Writing from Paris, Flora Lewis (IHT, 7-8 August) pinpointed the cause:

> The object of the battle is not a section of Beirut with arsenals stacked in crowded apartment houses. It is not even Lebanon . . . . It is correct, as a correspondent from Beirut wrote, that 'Operation Peace in Galilee' is an Israeli attempt to kill an idea, the idea of Palestinian nationality. Reports from Washington said US envoy Philip Habib was on the verge of getting a settlement when the latest Israeli attack was ordered. A compromise, without full humiliation of the PLO, would risk survival of the idea.

Civil Bombardment

The Israeli bombardment of Beirut can be roughly divided into four distinct phases during which it became increasingly heavy, widespread and indiscriminate. During the **first phase**, 4-24 June, the Israelis usually concentrated their aerial, naval and artillery fire on the southern suburbs of Khaldeh and Hay Saloum and the area south of the airport. Here casualties were, according to some reports, two combatants for every three civilians. There were, of course,

Palestinian prisoners held by the Israelis (AP)

many instances of bombing and shelling outside this area, particularly of traditional targets such as the Sabra and Shatilla refugee camps and the Fakhani area where the PLO had its operational headquarters.

On the 25 June Beirut suffered what was then called the 'worst bombing of the war', initiating the **second phase** which went on until 21 July. During this phase the Israelis extended the target area northwards, encompassing the airport and the refugee-slum suburbs of Ouzai and Bourj al-Barajneh. Here the ratio of civilian to combatant casualties became four to one.

The **third phase** began on 22 July with air raids on 'a new scale', a policy which was endorsed by the Israeli Cabinet after being presented by Sharon on the 25th as a new intensive, long-distance bombardment 'static fire' tactic. (Asher Wallfish in the *Jerusalem Post*, 26 July). On the 27th came the war's 'heaviest air and sea bombardment' to date, leaving 120 dead and 187 injured, in an enlarged target area extending to, and including, the Corniche Mazraa.

This phase ended on 31 July when Israel launched a prolonged onslaught on Ras Beirut proper — inaugurating the **fourth phase** — hitting massively and randomly at the commercial centre and residential districts which had been bombed earlier but so far spared concentrated attack. Here more than 90% of the casualties were civilians, many of whom were refugees bombed out of their homes and places of refuge during earlier phases.

Of this episode, which was not the last though the evacuation agreement was nearing completion, the American Ambassador to Lebanon, Robert S. Dillon, wrote in a confidential cable leaked to the press:

> Simply put, tonight's saturation shelling was as intense as anything we have seen. There was no 'pin-point' accuracy against targets in 'open spaces'. It was not a response to Palestinian fire. This was a blitz against West Beirut (*Sunday Times*, 8 August).

On 16 August J. Michael Kennedy (IHT) described what Israel had wrought in Beirut:

> This is a city of broken concrete, flattened apartment buildings and death. Once busy streets are now impassable because of rubble and shell craters. Whole neighbourhoods are gone. The products of lifetimes of work are gone, often obliterated in seconds by a 2,000 pound Israeli bomb . . . . In a little more than two months, the Israelis have inflicted damage in West Beirut . . . to a degree that makes the year and a half of civil war in 1975-76 seem almost minor.

All the bombardments were a 'blitz' against their victims.

> Amine and Kamel Mneimne were waiting patiently outside their old apartment building at 44 Farshoukh Street, off Basta Avenue, in central West Beirut. [Well outside the phase-one primary target area.] For four days they have been standing there, silently watching a bulldozer clear away the mountains of rubble where a three-storey building once housed their families . . . . They are looking for the remains of their wives, children and relatives still buried beneath the rubble. So far, 72 people have been dug out, all dead, and 12 others are missing and presumed dead . . . an Israeli bomb fell five minutes *after* the ceasefire between Syria and Israel at noon last Friday . . . . (David Ottoway in *The Guardian*, 12 June).

> A garage in the south Beirut district of Bourj al-Barajneh becomes home to 40 civilians and seven goldfish whenever artillery battles erupt between Israeli and Palestinian forces. For more than a month . . . it has been pressed into use as a shelter for civilians in that area [a target during phase two], most of them Lebanese but including some Palestinians (Reuter, 15 July).

> We actually saw the bomb, (wrote Robert Fisk *The Times*, 27 July). For a brief half-second, it hurtled down like a meteorite between two blocks of apartments on the sea-front at Raouche [outside the phase-three target area], and the explosion seemed to come from inside one's own head. We were covered in the fog of brown smoke and burning

dust that swept down the little hill, and only then did we hear the sound of the departing Israeli jet.

When we got to Iskandar Street half a building had been blown away, an eight-storey apartment block that had crumbled into a 10-ft-high pile of compacted concrete . . . . At the bottom of the street stood a middle-aged man with a moustache, whose perspiration streamed down his grubby shirt. 'There was nothing here to hit, only civilians,' he said . . . . If the Israelis intended to hit Iskandar Street, it was difficult to find a reason . . . . The most prominent residents were the Ambassadors of Canada, Switzerland, Yugoslavia and Greece, who could scarcely be regarded as targets.

On 29 July Fisk reported what was said about the raid by Theodore Arcand, the Canadian Ambassador, and the only senior Western diplomat to remain in Beirut until he was ordered out on 3 August.

'It is unbelievable that people are treated like this . . . . Eighty people were killed — so much for pin-point bombing.' Just before leaving Beirut, Arcand told the Associated Press that he and his staff had 'surveyed 55 separate areas in West Beirut that were hit in Israel's air, land and sea bombardment on 1 August. He said he considered none of them Palestinian military targets' (*Jerusalem Post*, 4 August). The destruction, he said, 'would make Berlin of 1944 look like a tea party' (*Sunday Times*, 8 August).

It was the Muslim feast of Id al-Fitr, marking the end of the month-long Ramadan fast. As the first light of day fell over West Beirut, families gathered to mourn their dead. Some people quietly prayed and read the Koran beside older graves marked by marble slabs and beribboned arbors. Others wept beside the many fresh mounds of dirt, marked only by cinder blocks. Nearby lay picks and shovels left by the gravediggers the evening before (*Time*, 2 August).

Charles T. Powers wrote in his 'Chronicle of a Bombardment':

By noon [on 2 August], residential areas on the east side of West Beirut were being pounded heavily [the total lack of discrimination marking phase four]. These were new targets for the Israelis, neighbourhoods occupied by the poor and working-class people of the city, overwhelmingly Muslim. Most of these people do not have the money to escape, or anywhere to escape to . . . . The bombardment . . . had been going on for almost nine hours without a lull (IHT, 3 August).

On 6 August Robert Fisk visited Rue Assi, where bombs had levelled two eight-storey blocks of flats: 'it looked as though an earthquake had hit the street'. Entombed were 'more than 100 people'. 'No one in this city is any longer safe from Israeli attack,' Fisk commented, 'no one and no area immune from air strikes or shelling . . . .' For example, 'the Lebanese Prime Minister's office stands only 250 yards from the ruined houses'. Then, in the early afternoon,

> a huge car-bomb – left at the end of Rue Assi – blew up, without warning, among the rescue workers, killing another eight people, including a pregnant woman . . . . The Israelis were to claim later that their aircraft hit PLO positions in Beirut after 'repeated ceasefire violations' (*The Times*, 7 August).

Then, on the 7th, a particularly frightening incident was reported by Alan Philps of Reuter:

> a lone Israeli warplane destroyed a six-storey apartment block in central West Beirut *with a single bomb* as Lebanese officials reported virtual agreement on evacuating trapped Palestinian guerrillas . . . . State-run Beirut radio said 100 to 150 people were killed or wounded . . . .
>
> Betna Mohabath wandered slowly down the scruffy alley, his skinny little legs stepping over chunks of concrete that had once been the walls of people's homes and trying to avoid the sharp edges of corrugated tin from collapsed roofing. In his arms were two bicycle wheels and a plastic bag with parts of a handle bar.
> He had been sent by his parents to help retrieve whatever was left from their bombed-out home in Bourj al-Barajneh . . . and his first concern had been that of any 10-year old boy – the remains of his bicycle.
> During the 10-week old Israeli invasion, Bourj al-Barajneh has received the longest and hardest pounding [of the three main Palestinian camps around Beirut] which formerly housed an estimated total of 80,000 Palestinian civilians, but are now uninhabitable (Robin Wright, *Sunday Times*, 15 August).
>
> About 40 people . . . most of them civilians have suffered serious burns from Israeli phosphorus bombs and shells, according to medical authorities in the city. Nearly half the victims are reported to have died from their wounds. Several hundred [such] shells have been fired into Beirut during the past fortnight, one of them hitting a Red Cross office (*The Times*, 2 August).

Israeli 'pin-point' shelling and bombing had other targets as well: they hit hospitals, killing people they had injured when they bombed them out of their houses. On 21 June, during what Anthony McDermott called Beirut's 'heaviest Israeli artillery and naval bombardment for a fortnight', shells fell on the Akka Hospital in south-east Beirut 'killing two people and injuring 13' (*Financial Times*, 22 June).

David Hirst went to the scene:

> Akka Hospital lies on the airport road. But it is hard to believe that last night's blitz was an accident, especially for an army of such professed efficiency . . . . 'We took 13 direct hits between 12:0 and 12:30 last night,' said Omar Sa-adi, a hospital official, who spent the night in the basement' (*The Guardian*, 22 June).

But that, as Robin Wright reported in the *Sunday Times* (4 July), was not the only hospital hit:

> 'Of all the unhappy civilians caught in the Lebanon, few can be as demoralised and despairing as the 800 men, women and children whose home was and is the Dar al-Ajaza Islamia Hospital in West Beirut.'
>
> 'The 800 are a mixture of senile geriatric patients, mentally retarded adults and children with mental problems.' Located in a residential area near the Palestinian camps of Sabra and Shatilla, the closest 'acceptable' target was the sports stadium 'half a mile off' where the PLO stored ammunition. Twelve naval and land-based artillery shells hit the hospital: 'Four . . . were phosphorus shells which scatter inextinguishable gobbets of burning chemical. Six patients were killed and 20 injured.'

In the Gaza Hospital nearby, the eastern exposure of the intensive-care room was sandbagged 'for fear of Israeli shelling from the hills to the east'. When it opened in the Sabra refugee camp in 1975 the hospital had 11 floors and 100 staff. In the first week of July it had seven surgeons and 12 beds and a kitchen which fed the neighbourhood 'where a handful of the poorest people in Beirut have remained' (James Buchan, *Financial Times*, 9 July).

On Sunday, 12 July, before the sixth ceasefire took hold at 9.45pm, the Israelis pin-pointed three hospitals, all further into town than the Akka, Gaza and mental hospitals in the southern suburbs. These were the Barbir, Makassed and Beirut hospitals. At the Barbir Hospital, which was bombed out floor by floor, ward by ward, in this and three subsequent attacks, Robert Fisk interviewed Dr Amal Shamaa:

> Probably the only hospital that has not been hit is the American University Hospital, but nearly every other hospital has been hit. This was deliberate.
>
> The Israelis know this hospital is here . . . even someone who is shelling from the sea or from the mountains can be more accurate than this.

Thirty per cent of the wounded were guerrillas; 21 casualties were brought in during the Sunday bombardment; in five weeks the hospital had received more than 200 dead (*The Times*, 13 July).

'If you are injured in war-torn West Beirut, don't bother to phone the city's ambulance headquarters', whose three vehicles were stolen in the early days of the war. 'Emergency aid is now provided by a motley and totally disorganised collection of ambulances run by everything from the [PLO] to the Red Cross.' Six engines at Beirut's main fire station had been knocked out of action by shell damage or mechanical breakdowns and two firemen were injured by cluster-bomb fragments soon after the invasion began (Thomas Thompson, Reuters, 28 July).

'Lebanese and foreign officials involved in emergency work are doubtful of ever being able to arrive at a final death toll figure from among the estimated half-million civilians who have spent nine weeks under Israeli [siege].'

But using figures compiled by Lebanon's Higher Relief Committee based on hospital data, 'Dr Kamel Mohanna, president of the Amel welfare association which has set up several emergency hospitals with overseas aid, put the toll at 5,000 dead and 15,000 wounded in Beirut from the time of the first air raids on 4 June, to the final 11 hours of bombing that ended on 12 August with the latest ceasefire' (Reuters, 20 August).

Blockade

Although the Israelis employed massive bombardment as their primary instrument for reducing West Beirut during the siege, their blockade of food and medical supplies and the cutting off of water and electricity inflicted more widespread suffering on civilians than did Israeli fire and brimstone. The formal blockade began on 3 July, after the population had suffered nearly a month's deprivation from extended power cuts and chronic water shortage. Many Lebanese, estimated at 100,000, crossed the 'green line' into East Beirut whether to leave for good or to rest and stock up on supplies before re-crossing into the western section during periods when the blockade was relaxed.

But the full force of blockade was enforced against the unfortunate civilians of Palestinian origin:

> Like the Jews trapped in the Warsaw Ghetto during World War II, many people living in besieged West Beirut are unable to flee because they belong to the wrong group. Because they are Palestinians they are turned back at checkpoints manned by the surrounding Israeli army or allied Lebanese Christian militia (Douglas Watson in the *Baltimore Sun*, 19 July).

Israel's policy of driving Lebanese civilians out of West Beirut while blockading Palestinian civilians inside explodes the myth — inspired by the Israelis — that the PLO was holding the people of Beirut hostage. The PLO did nothing to stop anyone from leaving; the only hostages in the city were the Palestinians kept there by the Israelis. The Lebanese who stayed did so

Bir Hassan, Beirut (Al-Safir)

because they wanted to, because West Beirut was their home or because they had no money and nowhere else to go.

The bombing and shelling enforced an informal blockade on Beirut for the first 10 days of the siege. During the first 48-hour truce negotiated by the US on 18 June, James McManus wrote, 'a lull descended on the battlefront' allowing 600,000 residents of West Beirut 'a day's relaxation . . . well-stocked shops raised their steel shutters for business'. There were no bread queues or panic buying, and fruit and vegetables came in, unhindered, from the north (*The Guardian*, 19 June).

But the city of half a million which was able to manage during lulls in bombing and shelling could not cope with the formal blockade Israel imposed, in a carefully prepared three-stage plan, on 3 July when food and fuel were cut off and on the 4th and 5th when electricity and water were shut off.

The Israeli army and its ally the Phalangist militia closed tight the two main crossing points from East to West Beirut on Saturday the 3rd, the Israelis assuming total control on Monday the 5th. 'At one roadblock Israeli soldiers confiscated sandwiches that someone wanted to take into the western part of town,' Silvi Keshet wrote in *Yediot Ahronot* (9 July), infuriated by the action of her own people.

The *Financial Times* carried a graphic description of the take-over of the power distribution and water pumping stations, an action denied by Col. Paul Kedar, the Israeli army spokesman in Beirut, until a public complaint was filed by the Lebanese Minister of Hydroelectric Resources, Mahmoud Ammar, a Shiite Muslim known for his anti-PLO views.

> Ammar and Musbah Natour, the electricity company's director general, said several Israeli soldiers entered the Karantina power control station on Sunday and ordered Lebanese workers to throw the switches that blacked out West Beirut . . . [Thereafter] three soldiers with automatic rifles, sleeping bags and food cookers stood guard in the control room.

Then on Monday afternoon, Ammar said,

> Israeli soldiers arrived at the Achrafiyeh water station and forced their way into the pumps. They shut the valves and dismantled the wheel, then hauled the wheel away. It is the key and the Israelis have it.

Within hours the situation became critical and dangerous. James McManus described (*The Guardian*, 6 July) how half a million people came 'to rely on saline water from wells, and stocks of canned food'. The contrast between the periods of informal and formal blockade was striking:

> Queues at water points have formed . . . and several fights have broken out among the heavily armed population and among the long queues of waiting women . . . Unicef has set up five [centres] for the distribution of bottled water but supplies are inadequate.

The food situation is also serious since loads of flour, which are usually taken by lorry from depots in East Beirut . . . have stopped completely. As in most Middle Eastern cities the flat Arab bread is a staple diet and its lack is keenly felt, especially in the poorer areas in the southern suburbs . . . .

The lack of clean water is causing health problems in a city whose hospitals are still crowded with the victims of shelling. The city's exhausted medical authorities . . . now report that cholera and typhoid have broken out in the poorer areas.

Doctors at the American Hospital here say that supplies of drugs are still holding out, but the Israeli blockade threatens to close the hospital since fuel supplies for the generators are down to four days.

By the 13th, 10 days after the medical supplies were blocked, Chris Drake reported (*The Guardian*):

The hospitals here . . . their staff already overworked, constantly appeal for the medical supplies they know to be waiting for delivery on the east side, but the Israelis have shown no signs of relaxing the blockade.

At Barbir Hospital, close to one of the checkpoints where people can cross, a doctor said victims were having to be transferred as soon as they arrived because there was no blood for transfusions during emergency operations . . . .

The shelling [of 12 July] was followed by fires which burned themselves out eventually because there was no water available to quench them.

On the 17th Drake reported (*The Guardian*):

crowds marched through the streets . . . yesterday, shouting protests against the food and fuel blockade imposed by the Israelis two weeks ago. But their protests appeared to make little difference. Some reports suggested that the Israelis reacted by tightening their stranglehold . . . preventing vehicles from leaving [West Beirut] for several hours.

He then listed the deprivations: 'stocks of canned food, gathered hurriedly when the invasion began six weeks ago, are running low, and there is a desperate shortage of fuel'; 'the Beirut municipality has announced formally that it is suspending rubbish collections indefinitely because there is no fuel for its trucks. It has asked people to burn rubbish in the streets to avoid outbreaks of typhoid;' 'more bakeries have closed, some because they do not have fuel, but others for lack of flour,' bags of which are 'too bulky to be smuggled through'.

On the 20th the Israelis relaxed the blockade of certain items, in limited quantities — drinking water, fruit, vegetables and flour — but allowed no fuel for the ovens so bakeries were 'largely unable to use the flour' they received. There were the inevitably daring taxi driver blockade runners who took the route through 'the ruins of Martyr's Square . . . with their cars full of fruit, fresh meat and fuel' (Robert Fisk, *The Times*, 21 July).

This relaxation, Jonathan C. Randall reported in the *Washington Post* (23 July), came at a time when the blockade, due to Lebanese business acumen and daring and the venality of Israeli soldiers manning the checkpoints (the bribe being $20), had become, 'with every passing day', increasingly 'porous'. 'Tomatoes, eggs, egg-plants, peaches, cherries, cucumbers, onions, apples, lettuce, mint are to be found in more than adequate supply . . . today [July 22] .

Refugee dwellings in Beirut (Al-Safir)

Prices, which zoomed to three or four times the normal . . . on 3 July, have now come back down . . . . Mutton, however, remains expensive . . . because the animals must be smuggled on foot through the lines . . . .'

The free-enterprise system prevailed, for those who still had homes and money with which to buy food. For the homeless and destitute the Israelis had shown no mercy. Until the 16th, 'the International Committee of the Red Cross was being allowed to bring in flour, powdered milk, sugar, dry beans, cooking oil, soap and basic kitchen utensils for displaced families. Suddenly the Israelis cut this off, apparently on instructions from the Israeli cabinet.'

During the weekend of 31 July-1 August the smuggling was stopped and the blockade was reimposed, with one further deprivation – the telephone by which West Beirutis kept in contact with friends and relatives in the world beyond the siege. On 5 August 'Israel, brushing aside US and United Nations appeals said . . . that it would not relax the siege of West Beirut' (IHT, 7-8 August).

On 6 August Reuter reported that 'Beirut was on the point of collapse, with food supplies fast running out and hospitals threatening to close'. Then on the 8th drinking water was restored for the first time in two weeks – but electricity remained off (IHT, 9 August). The water flowed – weakly, without pumps – for one week, before again being cut.

On the 10th Israel permitted a six-truck International Red Cross convoy into the city to deliver a field hospital and emergency rations – after the convoy had waited a day and a half 'to get approval . . . to pass the Israeli blockade' (IHT, 11 August). On the 12th Robert Fisk reported (*The Times*):

> Salma Sherif arrived at the bakery in Wadi Abu Jamil at 4am on Tuesday and left six hours later with just 10 pieces of flat Arabic bread. She paid 90p for the bread which will have to last her 13 children and nephews for two days. She has £40 left in family savings but when that runs out [her family] will starve – they are already drinking salt water . . . .

The Israelis eased their ban on fresh fruit and vegetables on 19 August, and on Sunday the 22nd, as the exodus of PLO fighters began, switched on the electricity necessary to pump the water throughout the city – which they promptly switched off again for some hours the next day because of procedural objections to the way the evacuation was being conducted.

In her *Yediot Ahronot* article of 9 July Silvi Keshet had commented sharply:

> 'Arik Sharon seems to have some sort of a recidivist connection with water. Wasn't it he, while serving as southern area commander, who stopped the bedouin's wells at the Rafah Approaches, in order to drive them away?' The blockade, she said, 'gives a new meaning to the words "cruel Zionism" '.

Sharon did not stop the water to drive the PLO away from Beirut, he did it simply to get his own way over the evacuation, in order that it should humble the PLO.

Psychological Pressure

The third instrument in Israel's siege strategy was psychological warfare. This campaign was conducted against the civilian population from the beginning of the siege, first by the bombing which drove the point home to Lebanese inhabitants of West Beirut that they should flee if they valued their lives and limbs. This is why, in particular, the Israelis made use of such terror weapons as cluster-bombs and phosphorus bombs.

The Israeli aim of clearing the city was emphasised on 28 July when they employed first one, then within hours a second, method of psychological pressure. First.

> Israeli aircraft passed over [the city], belching out what looked like pink smoke, then pink confetti, then pink and green leaflets which you had to catch in the hot draughty streets . . . . The leaflets warned, in bad but threatening Arabic, that people should leave towards the east or the north, as Israel had yet to use its full force against the Palestinian fighters (James Buchan and Nora Boustany, *Financial Times*, 29 June).

Such leaflets were dropped on a number of occasions: always issuing the threat of the final Israeli assault, which the Israelis never seriously considered launching. The threat of fighting the Palestinians in the streets was always just propaganda — to make people do what they wanted without having to fight.

Three hours after the first leaflets addressed to civilians were dropped a Renault-5

> parked in front of the offices of a group of French news organisations . . . blew up . . . [it was the last of eight that week]. The Palestinian Red Crescent was there in less than five minutes, the ambulances shrieking down the streets, the escort firing in the air to clear traffic. They went on firing for several moments more, perhaps to show they were keeping some sort of order but really out of fear — because the enemy could not be seen, but was at the south, and in the east, and perhaps among them already . . . Beirut had got the message (Buchan and Boustany, as above).

The leaflets and car-bombs were specific items on the agenda of the siege; then there were the tensions and terrors generated by the situation itself,

Arab University area of Beirut (Al-Safir)

and the fear of the dark. Anthony McDermott, looking back on his stay in Beirut during the first three weeks of the siege, wrote:

> The most immediate guide to the level of tension in beleaguered Beirut is the traffic. If the streets are empty — and at nightfall they are now almost totally deserted — then bombing and shelling, or the fear of it, cannot be far away. The strain is highest when the shells or bombs actually begin to fall. There is no longer any part of West Beirut which can be considered safe . . . .
>
> At night the tension can be particularly acute. When Israeli gunboats offshore launched sustained bombardments last week it was difficult to

assess initially whether the shells were being fired at random or were
part of a planned pattern.

There were random bursts of automatic firing — which may have reflected
'an excess of exuberance or just frustration at being stuck in a traffic jam.'
But people were killed in such incidents.

Then he mentioned the refugees, dispossessed and homeless, who brought
with them the aura of defeat and misery (*Financial Times*, 30 June).

The most important element of the psychological campaign was uncertainty. Robert Fisk summed it up (*The Times*, 24 July):

> No one thought they would return to raid the Lebanese capital again
> yesterday. But whenever an assumption is locked in stone, the Israelis
> have a way of breaking it open, at 1pm sharp yesterday they were
> here again . . . .

There was one thing that was predictable, however: that whenever it
looked as though a solution were near, the planes would return and the
gunners would resume their 'political bombardment'.

The Steadfast City

> Israel never intended that its forces enter Palestinian-held
> West Beirut during the Lebanese invasion, Prime Minister
> Menachem Begin told the Knesset Foreign Affairs Committee
> Tuesday [24 August].
> Israel Radio quoted Begin as telling the closed-door meeting
> that if Israel's position had been made public, the PLO would
> not have been pressured into leaving the city (Associated
> Press from Jerusalem).

What then did Israel intend? First, to drive the bulk of the Lebanese population out of the city in order to provide the Israelis with a free field of
fire against the PLO; second, to retain, through selective closing of the exits,
enough Palestinian civilian hostages to put pressure on the PLO to withdraw
on Israel's stringent, humiliating terms.

By the third week of July, the Israelis saw that their siege strategy had not
succeeded because the vast majority of Lebanese civilians would not leave.
So, like the Palestinians, they too became hostages to Begin's and Sharon's
ambitions to destroy the PLO structure and disperse its fighters. When
Sharon, on 25 July, declared all of West Beirut a 'static-fire zone', his object
was to put pressure on Habib, the American mediator, to mediate in his
favour.

But this final escalation of attacks on Beirut was not dictated by political
considerations alone. Sharon sought vengeance against the people of Beirut

who refused to be bombed, starved and terrorised into leaving their city. That is why the Israeli airforce struck out with its F15s and F16s in those last terrible days, with the full range of their weapons of mass destruction. Sharon wanted to cause the maximum suffering to the hapless and steadfast people of West Beirut. The Israelis secured the Palestinian evacuation they demanded, but they did not defeat the city they besieged.

4. Supporters and Dissenters

For the first time in Israel's 34 years of existence Israelis questioned the war their government was waging. David Shipler (*New York Times*, 20 June) said that they viewed the conflict as 'the first clearly initiated by Israel without major provocation and the first in which Israel's existence was not directly at stake'.

The first questioning of the war and the government's motives in starting it came within hours of the invasion army's entry into Lebanon, from both members of the Cabinet and the Labour opposition who had not been taken into the confidence of Prime Minister Begin and Defence Minister Sharon. The 'sole objective' of the attack, wrote Anthony Lewis (*New York Times*, 24 June), as explained by Israeli officials in both Jerusalem and Washington, 'was to clear PLO guerrillas from a 25-mile zone'. But 'when Israeli forces reached the 25-mile line, they did not stop for a minute'.

By the 10th, four days after the invasion began, ordinary Israelis began to express doubts about the war, and, what worried the Begin government most, soldiers on duty in Lebanon were among the first to ask uncomfortable questions. David Blundy described in the *Sunday Times* (1 August) the situation seven weeks into the war, after the opposition to the war had been building up following every escalation:

> Israel seems to be suffering an intensive bout of self-analysis, probing its own society, individual conscience and military obligation, free speech, patriotism and national ambition.

The key words were 'national ambition', for it was clear from the outset that the war was 'above all a victory for Sharonism', as Anthony Lewis had put it in his 24 June article.

> The Israelis who object to the war and its methods are a minority, and they are painfully aware of that fact. They see their country becoming Ariel Sharon's Israel and they despair.

What exactly does this mean? On the regional front,

General Sharon has made his strategic view clear. Apart perhaps from Egypt, he wants Israel to be surrounded not by stable, moderate Arab governments but by a power vacuum. He wants to destabilise King Hussein's Jordan, and his ambition reaches even to Saudi Arabia.

On the Palestinian front, Sharon simply seeks to crush Palestinian national identity. On that score, 'Janet Aviad, a sociologist, said of Israeli attitudes, "This country is in two camps — the people who want to talk to the Palestinians and the people who want to hit them. And the people who want to hit them have won".' (Shipler, as above).

The dissension led the Begin government and its supporters to take countermeasures, to launch a campaign to convince the doubters and waverers of the righteousness of their 'holy war'.

David Blundy reported (1 August) how the Israelis went about convincing certain sections of public opinion:

> It was a strange sight on a modern battlefield. As the F16s wheeled overhead and the missile boats stood offshore, a coachload of 40 Israeli and American rabbis arrived . . . on the hills overlooking Beirut. The Israeli government had arranged a conducted tour of the battle zone — a service already provided for US senators, congressmen, leaders of British Jewry, fund raisers and such film stars and singers as Jane Fonda and Sammy Davis Jnr.
> The religious front seems to have little doubt about the present war . . . The 40 rabbis agreed that the war was not only just but obligatory.

For less influential Jewish tourists, the Ministry of Tourism arranged briefing sessions at their hotels, presenting those who attended with colourful holiday postcards complete with a printed text describing the 'moving and enjoyable experience' for 'committed Jews' of 'travelling through Israel during the "Peace in the Galilee" campaign'.

On the internal front, pro-war groups — like the 'Voice of the Silent Majority' and 'Families of Terrorist Victims' — have sprung into action, charging dissenters with 'supporting the PLO' and being 'defeatists' and 'self-haters' (the *Jerusalem Post*, international edition, 4–10 July), the last an epithet usually reserved for anti-Zionist Jews. By 1 August David Blundy reported that 'pro-government forces were rallying' and had formed a pro-war 'Peace and Security Action Group' among intellectuals — '200 strong, and confident it will reach 2,000'.

On the popular level, the hawks had already demonstrated in their thousands and run advertisements in newspapers like the following:

> Citizens for Zahal.
> Lights on for Zahal.
> Our sons, husbands, brothers, friends and relatives are putting their lives on the line for us, while a vocal minority is sowing demoralisation.

Stop Defaming Operation Peace for Galilee.
Join us and demonstrate solidarity with Zahal. Drive with your lights
on all day, every day this week. (*Jerusalem Post*, 29 June).

Such morale-building was necessary because within Zahal, the armed
forces fighting in Lebanon, there was widespread criticism among the elite
units – the parachutists and commandos – and among the front-line troops
who saw the destruction of Lebanese towns and of Beirut with their own eyes.
'Most of the soldiers seem to have accepted the need to push the PLO guns
away from Israel's northern border,' wrote David Lennon from Tel Aviv
(*Financial Times*, 21 June).

'But what's the point of going up this far?' complained a reserve soldier.
. . . Another soldier on leave complained about the nature of this war.
'Up to now we fought armies and we knew who the enemy was. But how
do you relate to a 14-year-old kid with a gun whom you know you have
to shoot because he wants to shoot you? It's demoralising.'

A paratrooper, from a kibbutz and formerly a supporter of Begin,
stationed at Lake Karoun in the Bekaa Valley, wondered if this was the way
to solve the Palestinian problem.

'We do not have to come all the way to Beirut to look for PLO
guerrillas or sympathisers,' he says. 'They are sitting in our backyard in
the West Bank and Gaza Strip. . . . We know what they want, and we
know they won't be happy until we give them their state. Maybe that's
where we should be, sitting down with them and talking about a
Palestinian state.'

Lennon continued:

Many Israelis are also unhappy about the prospect of having to remain
in Lebanon for a very long time . . . Women whose husbands or sons
have returned from the fighting areas say their loved ones are depressed
and upset about the scale of destruction and the civilian casualties.
The rising casualty rate is also having its effect. There are burials
daily of soldiers who died in the fighting, which was supposed to have
lasted only a couple of days.

A 30-year-old parachutist from northern Israel wrote in the Israeli daily
Davar on 28 June:

From the start I did not agree with this mistaken move . . . I believe
that this was a war not forced upon us, by which ['those sitting at the
top' who 'wanted a war'] thought they can solve the Palestinian problem,
in a way that totally misses its point. This is true especially after taking

Tyre and Sidon we were given further options [to go to Beirut] . . . and that the only restriction would be external pressures.

In Sidon he found that the Israeli army's 'meeting with the population, after causing it so much misery and destruction, was one of the most shocking aspects of the war'.

Then he spoke of the rounding up of 'terrorists':

> Almost every Palestinian answers to the Israeli army's definition of a terrorist . . . it is unpleasant to compare, but if we look at Israel before the war of 1948, if you would go to a kibbutz everyone there was actually a Haganah member . . .

Almost all the members of the unit which carried out the Entebbe operation signed a protest against the war; so did 22 airforce pilots who, as a consequence, were rebuked by the Prime Minister in person; 92 reserve soldiers, who took part in this campaign, sent a letter to Defence Minister Sharon declaring their 'total lack of confidence' in him and in his 'military leadership', and demanding his 'immediate resignation' (published in *Ha'aretz, Davar* and *Al-Hamishmar*, 2 July).

A demonstration of reservists who had served in Lebanon took place in Jerusalem on 4 July: 122 of them, including 17 officers, presented a petition, signed in addition by several hundred soldiers, 'calling for an immediate end to the war' and for Sharon's resignation since he was responsible 'for a cynical use of the IDF without a national consensus'.

One of the leaders of this group, Moshe Savir, among the soldiers who took the Crusader castle of Beaufort, spoke out against the 'lying official reports' which said the castle was taken without 'any killed from our forces' and against radio broadcasts assuring Syrian forces that they would not be attacked while Israeli units were at that moment taking up positions to launch the attack. They called their movement 'Soldiers against Silence'.

There were open letters in the press from parents of the fallen. The most moving was from Ya'kov Guterman, of rabbinical descent, the only son of the Zionist socialist partisan Simha Guterman, who fell in the Warsaw Ghetto rising, father of Raz, the first to fall in the trenches before Beaufort. Ya'kov Guterman castigated the Begin government for seeking to 'unload . . . its incompetence' by 'achieving the doubtful glory of victors'.

> Cynically and shamelessly you declared the 'Peace for Galilee' operation when not one shot had been fired across the northern border for a year . . . my colossal sorrow . . . will pursue you in your sleeping and waking hours, and it will become the mark of Cain on your brows, for ever (*Ha'aretz*, 5 July).

There was another from Yehoshua Zamir, an immigrant from the US settled in the Galilee, whose son Yaron was also killed at Beaufort:

Is it our fate to live by the sword? A sword stained with the blood of babies? Has not the hour arrived to stop shooting and begin talking? . . . why should we not make a fair compromise with the Palestinian nation? (*Al-Hamishmar*, 1 July).

Among the pro-peace paraders was retired Lt.-Gen. Mordechai Gur, chief-of-staff during the 1978 invasion of Lebanon, who 'has emerged as one of the most vociferous critics of . . . Sharon's enlarged war aims' (Eric Silver, the *Observer*, 4 July).

At the front a 22-year-old first lieutenant, guarding one of the crossing points into West Beirut, told William Branigan (IHT, 12 July) it was 'his opinion that Israel "won't find a solution by war . . . You can't deny five million Palestinians. They have their rights".' Moses, a medical officer from Jerusalem, said that 'there had been cases of Israeli pilots refusing to bomb their targets because they were in populated urban areas . . . A young soot-smeared soldier assigned to a 175mm gun crew' asked reporters who had been in West Beirut 'how the other side feels about the war and whether it wants to continue fighting. "I want to stop," he said, "I want to go home".'

The soldiers' protest reached a climax when Col. Eli Geva requested that he be relieved of his command because of his doubts about the war. Geva, who led the attack on Sidon and whose brigade was then encamped near Beirut, was the son of a reserve general. Regarded as the hero of the campaign, Geva was sacked from the army at the end of July.

He was quoted by the daily *Yediot Ahronot* as telling his superiors:

> I don't have the courage to look bereaved parents in the face and tell them their son fell in an operation which in my opinion we could have done without.

Initially he was reported to have supported the invasion but 'doubts set in when the operation ballooned into an all-out effort to expel' the PLO from Lebanon (an Associated Press report in the IHT, 27 July).

To make their protest visible, in the third week of the war 'some soldiers from armoured units' set up a tent near the Prime Minister's office to mount a round-the-clock vigil against the continuation of the war. The movement 'is unprecedented at a time when tens of thousands of Israeli soldiers are in the battlefield and facing risk of death' (Christopher Walker, *The Times*, 29 June).

The most important group of politicians who, within 48 hours of the invasion, began to express misgivings about the actions and intentions of Begin and Sharon were fellow Cabinet members Mordechai Zipori (Communications), Zevlun Hammer (Education) and Yitzak Berman (Energy). Occasionally they were backed up by Simha Erlich (Deputy Premier and Agriculture) and Yosef Burg (Interior and Police).

Suspecting that Sharon was 'giving them only a partial picture' of the war, they 'insisted on knowing the aim' of the expanded operation. Zipori, Hammer and Berman constituted themselves as a watchdog committee to prevent Sharon from exceeding his brief (*Jerusalem Post*, international edition, 13–19 July). But the Cabinet did not succeed in putting the brakes on Sharon until the ninth week of the invasion, and then only at the insistence of the American President.

Other influential politicians who have criticised the war come from the ranks of the Labour Alignment – and then their criticism has been of the expansion of the campaign rather than the initiation of fighting. Among these were Shimon Peres, the Labour leader; Yitzak Rabin, former Prime Minister; and Abba Eban, former Foreign Minister and elder statesman. Peres criticised the use of the army for political rather than security ends and warned against the 'conquest of Beirut' (Eric Silver, *The Guardian*, 25 June). Eban called the siege of Beirut 'a dark age in the moral history of the Jewish people' (*Jerusalem Post*, 6 August).

Outright critics of the whole operation included Uri Avneri of the Sheli Party and the communists, who in the second week of the war tabled a no-confidence motion which was rejected by 94 votes to three.

More influential than the politicians but less than the soldiers were the intellectuals who from the outset opposed the war. On 12 June a group of Israeli academics, including retired Major General Mattityahu Peled, now Professor of Arabic at Tel-Aviv University,

> accused the government of launching an 'unjust war' and of 'deception' and charged that the IDF was 'slaughtering the Palestinians en masse'.

On the 13th the members of the newly-formed 'Committee against the War in Lebanon' demonstrated outside the Prime Minister's Office (*Jerusalem Post*, 13 June).

On the 20th a press conference was held by four of Israel's most distinguished intellectuals: Professor Yeshayahu Leibovitz, an organic chemist, philosopher and editor of the Hebrew edition of the *Encyclopaedia Hebraica*; Professor Dan Miron, Israel's foremost literary critic; Asa Kasher, Professor of Philosophy at the Hebrew University; and Nathan Zach, one of the most famous contemporary Hebrew poets.

Dan Miron said the present 'Peace for Galilee' operation reminded him of George Orwell's slogan in *1984*, 'war is peace'. Professor Leibovitz said that the war had resulted from the rising 'phenomenon of Judeo-Nazism' which had grown out of the conquest of the West Bank and Gaza in 1967. Professor Kasher considered the invasion an 'unjust war' which had as its result 'unjust deeds'. He criticised Begin's attempt to draw a parallel between Israel's campaign in Lebanon and the Allied campaign against the Axis powers in World War II.

Zach, the poet, was concerned about the state of Israeli society when he heard Israelis speak about 'the final solution' of the Palestinian problem.

I think that the man who began the war in Lebanon has such plans, that he has such a policy . . . I am afraid of the brutalisation and barbarisation which we are inflicting on ourselves. Thousands of us will return from the Lebanese war with wounded souls . . . I shudder when I see the men who represent me, Begin and his brutal troopers Sharon and Rafael [Eitan] (*Yediot Ahronot*, 21 June; *Kol Hair*, Jerusalem, 22 June; *Al-Hamishmar*, 22 June).

There followed more demonstrations and public protests by academics, scientists, poets and men of letters and frequent criticism by intellectuals in the daily press.

'A deeper analysis of the novel phenomenon of dissent . . . was given to the *Jerusalem Post* by Professor Hans Kreiter, a political psychology lecturer and friend of the late Zeev Jabotinsky,' the founder of Revionist Zionism, the movement which Begin follows. Kreiter wrote:

All our wars from 1948 to 1973 were over the very existence of statehood . . . This was the first time that this was not the case. True, the official PLO line has been to dismantle Israel, but no one felt that they had the power to do it.

The questioning began, he said, before the invasion when the army was asked to shoot at demonstrating West Bank Palestinians. And the questioning 'was deepened' by speculation on whether the cost in human lives has been too great (reported by Christopher Walker in *The Times*, 22 June).

One of the things which caused a flurry of criticism among intellectuals was the reply sent by Begin to President Reagan's cable greeting him on his birthday. Begin tried to draw a historical parallel between the destruction of Beirut in 1982 and of Berlin in 1944:

I feel as a prime minister empowered to instruct a valiant army facing Berlin where, amongst innocent civilians, Hitler and his henchmen hide in a bunker deep beneath the surface.

One reaction was that Begin was 'living in a surreal world' and 'fighting the Warsaw Ghetto all over again'; a teacher of holocaust studies in Jerusalem described Begin's message as 'a dangerous and delusionary analogy' (*Sunday Times*, 8 August). Naomi Kies, who teaches political science at the Hebrew University, an active member of the committee against the war, drew another sort of parallel with the holocaust:

I remember the first time we saw on Israel TV a little boy coming out of the rubble with his hands up. People asked, 'Is he holding his hands up to us?' It recalled a holocaust picture we wanted to forget (James Feron, IHT, 24 August).

26 June: demonstration in Tel-Aviv (Gamma)

Scholars helped to organise a series of mass protests, like that on 3 July in Tel-Aviv which attracted 100,000 Israelis to call for an immediate halt to the war and the resignation of Sharon (*Jerusalem Post*, 5 July). It was 'one of the largest organised by the Peace Now movement for nearly four years', reported Christopher Walker in *The Times* (5 July).

> Prominent among the protesters were a number of reserve officers who had recently returned from the front line . . . The rally was seen as a defiant answer to an opinion poll published 24 hours earlier which showed that 93 per cent of the Israeli public supported the war.

Ian Black summed it up (the *Guardian*, 5 July):

> The peace camp is no longer just against war. It wants peace — and peace with the Palestinians. The soldiers and civilians who demonstrated in Tel-Aviv . . . carried a message that will echo far beyond the aftermath of this war. 'Enough! We can no longer ignore the other people who claim this sad land for their own.'

This was the largest of the anti-war demonstrations. It followed one of 20,000 again in Tel-Aviv the preceding week. Two weeks after the massive Peace Now rally, a pro-war demonstration, attended by the Prime Minister, drew 250,000 (IHT, 9 August).

Begin and Sharon dismissed the protest as 'fringe opinion' (Christopher Walker, *The Times*, 5 July) and said it would have no effect on policy; in Beirut, Sharon called press reports of dissent the troops' 'daily dose of poison' (Christopher Walker, *The Times*, 29 June). The fact was, however, that the doubts about the war which blossomed into vociferous opposition did worry the government and did have an impact on the general climate of public opinion in Israel towards the invasion of Lebanon. On 15 July P. Sever wrote in *Al-Hamishmar*: 'Because the people already know the truth, we have lost the war.'

But while an influential segment of Israeli public opinion came to condemn the war, and Cabinet colleagues grew to observe Begin and Sharon with increasing suspicion, Washington's support for the military aspect of the operation was never seriously diluted by its condemnation of the death and destruction it wrought. Indeed, as Hanna Semer of *Davar* said in an interview with Frederick Kempe (*Wall Street Journal*, 18 June), 'American support for Mr Begin's actions made opposition [by Israelis] all the more difficult.'

'War is Peace' in Washington

As popular protest against the war grew in Israel, in Washington the Reagan administration simply refused to put enough pressure on the Begin government to stop the invasion, or even to relieve the siege of Beirut, which President Reagan was not moved to do until the two massive aerial bombardments in August — and even then the bombardment was halted only after the second intervention. The Reagan administration, from the first days of the war; covered its inaction — which under Alexander Haig's management amounted to collusion — with slogans which were then taken up by the Washington establishment, including the press.

Secretary of State Haig launched the sloganeering with the phrase 'a great strategic opportunity'; then elaborated with 'the chance for drawing a new political map of the region'. Some spoke of 'creating a strong central government in Lebanon', presumably as the phoenix which would rise out of the ashes of the greater part of Beirut. Henry Kissinger said that the invasion had 'created opportunities for American diplomacy'. Others among Haig's partisans spoke of 'breaking the stalemate in Middle East diplomacy' and of 'creating conditions for a lasting peace in the area'.

Anthony Lewis, in 'Combing the Wreckage' (*New York Times*, 10 June), wrote: 'The fatuous optimism of [such] views would make Dr Pangloss blush . . . . In fact, the Israeli operation is reducing the influence of the United States.'

The Times in London, in its editorial of 23 June, said that

> The opportunity can be seized only if America demonstrates her willingness and ability to restrain Israel's ambitions. Israel must not be allowed to redraw the political map of the area to suit her own taste, and the United States is the only power which can stop her.

But American policy on the invasion was always Alexander Haig's policy — even after his resignation on 25 June and George Shultz's succession three and a half weeks later. Ten days before the invasion Haig met with Sharon. Later Sharon gave an interview, quoting 'from his notes on conversations in Washington'. He said he had told Haig, 'Our aim is not to set up an independent Lebanon or to get the Syrian forces out of Lebanon.' (Both of which, perhaps, he decided to undertake at a later date.) 'We cannot live under the threat of Palestinian terrorism from Beirut. We do not see any alternative but to go there and clean up. We don't want you to be surprised. But we don't know when it will happen' (*Jerusalem Post*, 30 June).

Thus Sharon made it very clear to Haig that Israel would invade Lebanon and its forces would go all the way to Beirut. Haig saw in the situation Israel would create in Lebanon 'a great strategic opportunity' for the US to reconstitute Lebanon without the presence of 'an international terrorist organisation' in Beirut (IHT, 6 July). He saw this opportunity as 'America's moment in the Middle East' (*The Times*, editorial, 23 June). He saw it also as his own personal strategic opportunity to get ahead in politics: the idea of becoming President of the United States appealed to him (Robert Chesshyre, the *Observer*, 27 June) and a major foreign-policy success would have brought this goal nearer.

Alexander Haig was one of the few American policy-makers who got on well, on a personal level, with Menachem Begin. Indeed the two men had formed a sort of mutual admiration society which they described in separate interviews during Begin's visit to Washington in June with Trude B. Feldman (published in the IHT on 6 and 7 July). Asked about their relations, Begin said,

> When we first met in Israel [in July 1974, during a visit to Israel by President Nixon] we sat together at the same table and talked for close to three hours. From then, I drew the conclusion that Mr Haig is a great patriot, a man who loves freedom, a man who will always defend liberty. And when he became Secretary of State a very warm personal rapport was established between us. Israel does not have a better friend in the United States or any other country.

If Begin's attitude was admiration, Haig's was one of deep sympathy for Israel, and for Begin. Haig was asked how Begin's visit to Washington went. Were there any provocations? 'Mr Begin never provokes me. I think I know where he comes from. He is a patriot. He is a man who is isolated, as are his people, in an unfriendly environment . . . He is a leader with a great burden.'

The fact that Haig had been forewarned of Israel's intentions by Sharon, combined with the closeness of his relationship with Begin, made him confident he could handle the situation produced by the invasion. It perhaps led Haig to be selective when he briefed the President about his meeting in May with Sharon. The President always insisted later that he had no fore-knowledge of the Israeli decision to enter Lebanon.

During a press conference on 30 June Reagan said in answer to a question: 'We were not warned or notified of the invasion that was going to take place.' And later he said: 'We were caught as much by surprise as anyone' (quoted by Joseph C. Harsch, the *Christian Science Monitor*, 11 July). Reagan's royal 'we' meant the administration, which was wrong because Haig knew.

In answer to accusations made by several Arab governments, Reagan said during this press meeting, 'I have given no green light [for the Israeli attack] whatsoever' (Reuter, 1 July). Reagan may not have given a formal 'green light' but Haig certainly did not flash a 'red light' in the ten days before the invasion. Furthermore Haig's possible, even probable, duplicity over Sharon's advance warning does not excuse Reagan, who should have been informed of the build-up of Israeli forces along the border and who had two and a half days after the advance aerial bombardment began to put a stop to the invasion which was then imminent.

But Reagan, who was attending the economic summit meeting at Versailles, did nothing until just 10 hours before the Israelis crossed the border. Only on 6 June,

> at 7 am Jerusalem time, after the decision had been made to launch the invasion, was a letter from the President, sent from Versailles about six

hours earlier, delivered by messenger to Mr Begin. An Israeli official said that the United States Embassy had tried to reach Mr Begin during the night with the letter but that Mr Begin had been unavailable (David Shipler, *New York Times*, 7 June).

This slowness to act was certainly taken by Begin and Sharon (who must have thought Haig had certainly told the President what Sharon had said in May) as a green light and must be considered as such by anyone trying to assess American policy on this issue.

Anthony Lewis (*New York Times*, 10 June) gave an explanation for Reagan's delayed action, an explanation which further discredits the administration:

As Israel bombed and then invaded Lebanon, the Assistant Secretary of State for Near East and South Asian Affairs, Nicholas Veliotes, was on vacation. The National Security Council's staff specialist on the region, Geoffrey Kemp, was also away. [Thus] President Reagan delayed sending a message . . . until the day of the invasion. That was American leadership. That is why Israel treats American views with indifference bordering on contempt.

Thus the stage was set, with Begin, Sharon and Haig playing leading roles, while Reagan, uninformed and totally preoccupied with his European tour, had a mere supporting role. The administration did what was expected, pro forma, calling on 5 June for a ceasefire and on the 6th, at the United Nations Security Council, for the 'immediate withdrawal' of Israeli forces. The White House Deputy Press Secretary claimed that the US had 'pulled out all the stops . . . to halt the fighting'. But if it had, the length of the fighting would have been measured in hours, rather than days, weeks and months.

Although Israel was clearly not heeding Washington's demands, 'US officials appeared reluctant to criticise Israel', and were totally unwilling to exert pressure on Israel by any of the means available. Haig, when 'asked whether it was legitimate for Israel to use aircraft and tanks supplied by the US, replied: "These are questions of extreme importance, questions on which assessments will be made in the hours ahead . . ."' Haig refused to say whether the administration agreed with the condemnation of Israeli violence issued by President Francois Mitterrand of France on behalf of the seven nations represented at the summit' (which ended on the 6th).

In New York at the UN, US Ambassador Jeane Kirkpatrick adopted the line which became characteristic of all her subsequent utterances before the Security Council: she said it would 'not be reasonable or balanced or fair simply to point a finger of blame' at Israel (*Financial Times*, 8 June).

In Washington 'the State Department said that Israel "will have to withdraw its forces from Lebanon" but it refrained from criticising the assault against military bases of the [PLO]'. Defence Secretary Caspar Weinberger, in a television interview, 'declined to say whether the Reagan administration was considering a suspension of arms shipments or any other form of sanction against Israel for its invasion' (Bernard Weinraub, *New York Times*, 8 June). Meanwhile, in Lebanon Israeli planes bombed Tyre, Sidon and Beirut and Israeli tanks rolled on northwards.

To be fair, the wait-and-see attitude adopted by the administration, both in Washington and among officials touring Europe with the President, may have been due to the fact that both the President and his staff — with the exception of Haig — believed the Begin government's statements about the limited scope of its operation. These statements were believed, after all, even by informed observers in Jerusalem, like the editors of the *Jerusalem Post* who, on the morning of 8 June, printed the headline: 'Tyre, Beaufort fall as IDF operation nears completion'.

Even the Israeli Ambassador in Washington was, apparently, kept in the dark about the intentions of Begin and Sharon. On the 7th he told reporters in a meeting at the Israeli Embassy: 'I think we're well on the way to establishing our objective — to remove the rocketry and artillery of the PLO out of range of Israel's towns and villages' (Bernard Weinraub, *New York Times*, 8 June).

On 8 June President Reagan mentioned the Middle East in his address to the British Parliament, saying that 'the fighting . . . must stop and Israel should bring its forces home'. Echoing Haig's form of words in reference to the PLO, he said, 'We must all work to stamp out the scourge of terrorism that in the Middle East makes war an ever present threat.'

At a press conference Haig said that 'the President had deferred judgement on whether Israel's use of American arms in Lebanon constituted justified self-defence or a form of aggression that would violate American law'. He told the British Foreign Secretary that 'a key American aim would be a strengthening of the Lebanese government' and 'as part of a comprehensive solution "we would hope there would be some lessening of [the] Syrian presence".' (Hedrick Smith, *New York Times*, 9 June). Thus Haig declared his ambition to effect 'a comprehensive solution', on the second day of the invasion, at a time when other informed observers thought the Israeli action would soon be over.

On 9 June, during a flight from London to Bonn, Haig said that the US had 'expressed its concern' to Begin that Israeli forces had advanced into Lebanon 'well beyond the 25-mile limit originally mentioned by the Israeli cabinet'. His comments appeared to imply that the US was 'less worried' about the first 25 miles than the extension beyond, which, however, Haig said, 'might be described as "tactical and not necessarily strategic".' He admitted that if Israel's aim was to be accomplished, the timing of the 'withdrawal of its forces was going to be difficult' (Reginald Dale, *Financial Times*, 10 June).

These remarks make it clear that Haig had already begun to whittle down the administration's initial, pro forma, demand for immediate Israeli withdrawal and to suggest that Israel had objectives beyond the 25-mile security zone in south Lebanon.

Then at another press briefing, on 9 June in Bonn, Haig laid the blame for the extension of Israel's military action directly on Syria. David Landau reported in the *Jerusalem Post* (10 June) that Haig had confirmed that 'Syria [had] deployed "a rather substantial number" of additional anti-aircraft missiles in the Bekaa Valley' since the invasion began. 'It was this Syrian reinforcement of the missiles that prompted Israel to send in the IAF [Israeli airforce] to attack them, Haig told newsmen.'

That night in the Security Council the US vetoed a Spanish-sponsored draft resolution which condemned Israel's refusal to withdraw from Lebanon and threatened it with sanctions. Mrs Kirkpatrick explained the veto by saying that the draft was 'not sufficiently balanced to accomplish the objective of ending the cycle of violence'. Zoriana Pysariwsky wrote (*The Times*, 10 June): 'The United States stood alone in opposing the draft and left itself vulnerable to accusations that it condoned the Israeli invasion.'

Then, on the 10th,

> Washington's tacit backing for the massive Israeli invasion . . . appeared to come to a sudden halt at 2 am . . . when Mr Samuel Lewis, the US Ambassador in Tel Aviv, arrived at the Jerusalem home of Menachem Begin. . . . He brought an urgent message from President Ronald Reagan demanding that Israel stop fighting in Lebanon immediately . . .
>
> At 4 am, as dawn was breaking over the Middle East, two events occurred simultaneously: the Israeli airforce renewed its bombing of Beirut, and Mr Begin informed his cabinet ministers of the US demand to halt the fighting.
>
> At 7 am Mr Lewis was received again by the Israeli Premier, who gave him Israel's first reply to the Reagan demand. The . . . contents have not yet been released, but the Israeli armoured columns indicated the response by pressing on [with their attacks].

During the cabinet meeting, convened at 9 am, Begin spoke to Haig on the telephone and suggested he visit Jerusalem that day, and Haig agreed. By 1 pm Lewis gave a second message to Begin from Reagan demanding compliance. Begin replied that he would discuss terms for a ceasefire only when Haig arrived in Jerusalem. Reagan declined to send Haig, and the fighting continued (David Lennon, *Financial Times*, 11 June).

Begin had showed his hand: he was prepared to give to the Secretary of State — after some discussion, and at the price of a visit to Jerusalem in war-time — what he would not grant the President. A furious Reagan apparently withdrew from centre-stage after this personal defeat administered by Begin, and Haig took over the handling of the crisis.

Unhindered by the unwanted advice of less staunch supporters of Israel (like the Defence Secretary and the National Security Adviser), Haig followed a firm line in the direction of his 'strategic opportunity' policy. On 13 June, on American television, Haig avoided calling for an immediate withdrawal of Israeli troops. Instead he said, 'I think we are going to want and [will] work to achieve . . . a withdrawal of all foreign elements [the PLO and the Syrians as well as the Israelis] ' (*Wall Street Journal*, 14 June).

On 14 June, Haig announced: 'It is our hope that the ultimate solution to the Lebanon crisis will be a catalyst for facilitating progress in the peace process, rather than an obstacle to progress.' Palestinian autonomy talks, announced Haig, were linked to the 'resolution of the situation in Lebanon' (*Al-Fajr* weekly, 18–24 June).

On the same day a senior US official at the UN conveyed to other members of the Security Council that 'the demand for unconditional Israeli withdrawal was "no longer adequate to the needs of the situation". He pointed instead to the activities of the special US envoy to the Middle East [Philip Habib] . . . who was in Beirut . . . seeking a basis for strengthening the Lebanese government' (Don Oberdorfer and John M. Goshko, *The Guardian*, 16 June).

Then, on the 16th, Haig linked a revival of the autonomy talks to the disappearance of the PLO from the Lebanese scene, saying that 'it was not in the US interest to see the PLO reconstituted there' because it posed a threat to the autonomy negotiations which the PLO condemned (*Al-Fajr*, 18–24 June).

Thus, within a week, elements of Haig's design had begun to emerge: the expulsion of the PLO from Lebanon and the withdrawal of the Syrians; the creation of a Lebanese government capable of policing its territory and policing the Palestinians who remained there; and the imposition of 'autonomy' on the Palestinian inhabitants of the Israeli-occupied West Bank and Gaza, disregarding their demand for self-determination.

The *New York Times*'s diplomatic correspondent, Bernard Gwertzman, commented on US policy fluctuations (18 June):

> At the end of last week . . . the administration shifted priorities and . . . tried to work parallel to the Israelis to achieve a long-term solution that would produce a new situation in Lebanon more favourable to Israeli interests . . . Mr Haig and others also decided that the shock to the Syrians and the Palestine Liberation Organisation in Lebanon created a chance for drawing a new political map in the region.

But, according to Gwertzman, Haig did not get his way with all the American officials concerned:

> Philip C. Habib. . . has had some disputes in recent days with Mr Haig over the position to take toward the Israelis . . . Mr Habib has advocated a stronger line with the Israelis, saying that he feels their military actions in the Beirut area have been out of proportion to the military need.

Habib was not alone in his criticism of Haig's handling of the siege of Beirut; it became, within days, the focus of opposition to Haig's policy, and to Haig personally, both in the Department of State and elsewhere in the administration. Bernard Gwertzman wrote on 20 June (*New York Times*, 21 June):

> Prime Minister Menachem Begin of Israel arrives here today for talks
> with President Reagan amid signs that the Reagan administraion was
> divided on how to react to Israel's moves in Lebanon . . . the President
> was receiving conflicting advice from high-ranking advisers . . .

Haig, officials said,

> advocates a soft public approach to Mr Begin. Two other senior aides,
> William P. Clark, the National Security Adviser, and Defence Secretary
> Caspar W. Weinberger, were said to favour a public rebuke.
>   Mr Weinberger made clear today that he strongly opposed the
> Israeli military moves. He said it was incorrect to assume that Mr Haig,
> who refused to criticise Israel, was speaking for the administration . . .
>   Commenting on the State Department [i.e. Haig's] view that the new
> situation in Lebanon created an opportunity for the United States to
> work out a diplomatic solution in the Middle East, Mr Weinberger
> said . . . 'I don't think we can ever be in the position, as a government,
> of condoning or supporting or blinking at the idea that you can or
> should change the status quo by unilateral resort to military force. . . .
> The United States condemned Argentina for the same act of force.'
>   In the strongest criticism by an administration official of the Israeli
> action, he said Mr Begin should have limited his actions to diplomacy
> and not used force in Lebanon . . . 'But when you just send in columns
> of tanks and kill civilians [who] have nothing whatever to do with it,
> then I would say the [political] process has failed and it is time to
> start over, with our opposition to that kind of thing clearly understood.'

Weinberger suggested that the President was working on a new policy. He
had already established a 'special situation group' under Vice-President
George Bush to monitor the Middle East crisis. There were indications that
Begin's meeting with Reagan might be cancelled, as an expression of American
displeasure over Israel's actions. It looked, at that moment, as if Haig's
opponents were winning in the battle for the President's ear. Haig then had
the backing of only two prominent members of the administration – UN
Ambassador Kirkpatrick and Arms Control and Disarmament Agency Director
Eugene Rostow (*Jerusalem Post*, 27 June).
    It was decided that the meeting would go ahead as scheduled. An hour
before, Reagan met with his advisers, with apparently nothing decided. The
IHT reported (22 June) that 'there was no clear sign that the White House
had made a decision on how to react to Israel's invasion of Lebanon'.
Obviously Begin made a favourable impression on the President because
'Mr Begin not only escaped public criticism by the President, but also emerged
. . . with broad agreement about long-term objectives in Lebanon' (Nicholas
Ashford, *The Times*, 23 June).

. . . Mr Reagan [had] rejected Weinberger's advice that he cut military aid to Israel or at least denounce the Israelis in public. In doing so, Mr Reagan ran the risk of seeming to endorse the Israeli invasion and possible Israeli moves to crush the Palestinian forces in Beirut. The officials said Mr Reagan, personally sympathetic to Mr Begin's security concerns for Israel, agreed with the assessment of . . . Haig that a public attack on Israel during Mr Begin's visit would be counterproductive and lead only to Israeli inflexibility.

Then, during lunch at the White House, Reagan 'read a virtual riot act to Begin' (Robert Chesshyre, the *Observer*, 27 June) over the bombardment of civilians in Beirut and 'declined to toast his guest'. (Harold Jackson, *Guardian*, 28 June).

Reagan secured from Begin a pledge that the Israelis would not overrun Beirut (which they had no intention of doing anyway, but which they were threatening to do) and had the White House press secretary make it public. (Chesshyre, above). Begin reneged, however, by publicly declaring his refusal to comply with the administration's wishes; at a meeting with leaders of American Jewish organisations he said Israel 'would not respond to "friendly pressure" to give up pursuit of the PLO' (Zoriana Pysariwsky, *The Times*, 22 June) — even into Beirut. On the Beirut front, firing and bombardment resumed less than 24 hours after Habib's latest ceasefire.

Begin returned to Jerusalem claiming 'to have secured the "profound understanding" of Haig for "Israel's position".' (Christopher Walker, *The Times*, 24 June). Haig was the last member of the administration to meet with Begin before his departure: perhaps this 'profound understanding' was reached then. It led Haig to scuttle an American peace plan being negotiated by the 'special situation group' and William Clark, Reagan's National Security Adviser, involving Saudi Arabia's King Fahd in Riyadh and, via Fahd, with Arafat in Beirut. On Wednesday the 23rd Fahd phoned Arafat to confirm that an 'honourable solution' had been worked out. Later in the day, however, Habib transmitted to Arafat, unexpectedly, a long list of questions and 'insisted he must have written answers'.

'On Thursday [the 24th] . . . Arafat delivered the answers in the form of a multi-page memorandum, reaffirming his guarantee to end all PLO military activity in Lebanon.' It was expected that Habib 'would formally endorse the truce. But . . . he stalled, while Israel's land, sea and air bombardment of the city rose to new heights.'

Apparently Haig had got wind of 'what was being cooked up by Clark, Fahd and Arafat — and didn't like it even though Reagan himself was . . . behind it . . . [But] Habib answers directly to the Secretary of State.' Who else could have sent 'the signals that caused Habib to delay'?

'The net result . . . was that the peace plan died and Habib was instructed to represent the maximalist Israeli position as official US

26 June: demonstration in Tel-Aviv (Gamma)

policy – an order against which he reportedly submitted an official protest' (the *Sunday Times*, 27 June).

If the plan of the 'special situation' group had been allowed to succeed, the war would have ended at the beginning of its third week. The PLO had agreed, in principle, to leave Beirut – and King Fahd, its most important financial backer, was committed to see that it did. All that remained was to decide how, when and where the PLO would go (it had already been decided that those who left would include the entire military wing and the top leadership).

This should have suited Israel if the Begin government had held to the stated objective of the invasion – the elimination of the PLO 'security threat' from Beirut. But Begin, and his friend Haig, had their larger, secondary objectives to protect. A negotiated settlement did not suit them at this point, nor did the notion that the PLO would be allowed to make an 'honourable' retreat. So Haig subverted the peace plan from within the State Department.

By doing so Haig shifted the responsibility for its failure away from Israel, as Begin was certain to reject it, thus making worse his already strained relationship with Reagan, who backed the plan. Haig thereby personally prolonged the siege of Beirut, intensifying the sufferings of its population. (More than four-fifths of the civilians who died, some 4,000 people, died after 23 June.)

The last two tasks Haig performed as Secretary of State were less important. On Friday the 25th, the day of Haig's resignation, Reagan became so concerned about the escalation of Israel's attacks on Beirut that he considered telephoning Begin 'to demand a personal assurance that Israel would cease fire'. Haig advised against it and called on the Israeli Ambassador in Washington, securing a ceasefire a few hours later. In addition, it was reported that the administration had warned Arab governments 'that it could not guarantee continued Israeli observance of the . . . truce unless [the PLO] laid down its arms' (Harold Jackson, *The Guardian*, 29 June).

Later Haig instructed the US delegation at the UN to veto a French-sponsored Security Council resolution calling on Israel to withdraw from Beirut. It remained Haig's view that Israel must be given time to apply enough military pressure to make the PLO forces leave (see Alex Brummer, *The Guardian*, 25 June) and leave on Israel's tough terms.

Haig also tried to impose his policies on the administration during the interregnum between his resignation as Secretary of State and the Senate confirmation of his successor, three and a half weeks later. On 30 June the Israeli government received a long letter from Häig 'setting down US policy principles regarding Lebanon, which are for the most part "almost identical", according to Israeli sources, with Israel's own positions' (David Landau in the *Jerusalem Post*, 1 July). Haig certainly deserved the regard of Israeli policy-makers 'as the prime mover in Washington's support for – or at least condoning of – "Operation Peace for Galilee".' (The *Jerusalem Post*, 27 June).

Haig's legacy was the continuation of the war and the policy of 'strategic opportunity'. The Reagan administration could neither halt the fighting in Lebanon nor free its mind of the slogans which led it to believe the crisis might have a 'silver lining'.

With Shultz's appointment the administration had a golden opportunity to adopt a more even-handed policy towards the crisis. Indeed some observers in Washington were predicting an abrupt switch to public criticism of Israel and the threat, or actual imposition, of sanctions. Early in the war Israel had begun to lose the support of the American people. The chairman of the House Foreign Affairs Committee noted a 'diminished' support for Israel in Congress (*New York Times*, 10 June), and a 'rising antipathy' was becoming apparent on the popular level 'toward Menachem Begin's belligerence' which 'could eventually poison US attitudes toward Israel and thus jeopardise its future'.

Although this trend 'was visible' before the invasion, 'it has been accelerated by newspaper accounts and television scenes dramatising Israeli aggressiveness toward innocent civilians. An important distinction marks the picture. Surveys constantly show that a majority of Americans believe that the United States must remain committed to Israel. An increasing proportion, though, have become critical of Begin' (Stanley Karnow in the IHT, 22 July).

But at the moment when Haig's actions were most criticised, Bernard Gwertzman wrote about a pro-Israel shift in a part of the administration (*New York Times*, 24 June): 'Now, the Israelis seem to be getting a more sympathetic reception from the executive branch, which feels (or has begun to feel) that Israel's move into Lebanon has provided the possible basis for breaking the stalemate in Middle East diplomacy.'

Thus Haig's policy outlived his departure. Indeed Reagan's first action after Haig's resignation was to assure America's friends and allies of the continuity of US foreign policy. This continuity was assured by two political factors and by several of Reagan's own personal characteristics. The first factor was Israel's readiness to use military force against West Beirut to get what it wanted. The second was that no one in the administration was prepared to tackle Begin. During most of the crisis it was Begin who dictated to the Reagan administration how and when he would be approached by them, rather than the other way round.

The *Washington Post*'s Jerusalem correspondent (in an article published in the IHT, 17 August) wrote about the difficulties of dealing with Begin: '. . . while Mr Begin will act when confronted with an angry President . . . any action that goes beyond threats and angry words is bound to produce an unpredictable but counterproductive Israeli response'.

Then there was the President himself. Reagan's own political views on the invasion were a mirror image of those held by the opposing camps in his administration. He was 'torn between instinctive sympathy for Israel and increasing shock at the civilian casualties and worldwide alarm caused by Israel's invasion of Lebanon.' (*Time*, 12 July). Both during his campaign and as President he had always spoken of the PLO as a 'terrorist' organisation.

On the personal side, he was known to prefer 'tranquillity' (Robert

Chesshyre, the *Observer*, 27 June); he 'abhors conflict among his subordinates'. For the 18 months Haig had 'reigned as vicar of American foreign policy', Haig had had his way because the President, as William Quandt, former National Security Council adviser on the Middle East, observed, 'doesn't like arguments' (the *Sunday Times*, 8 August).

'To describe [Haig] as prickly is to abuse the language,' wrote Harold Jackson (*The Guardian*, 28 June). He only had to threaten a scene to get his way. Obviously Begin took his cues from Haig (whom he had seen two days earlier) in his talks with Reagan on the morning of 21 June.

Reagan's decision to accept Haig's resignation was a painful one because it disturbed the atmosphere. Reagan's preference for tranquillity, his political predilections and his administration's reluctance to administer more than a private verbal rebuke to Begin led to the adoption of a soft line towards Israel's increasingly brutal campaign. This hampered Habib's efforts to get the violence stopped.

Anthony Lewis summed it all up in an article in the *International Herald Tribune* on 6 August:

> During [the 1 August] bombing of Beirut, President Reagan said he had 'lost patience [with Israel] a long time ago'. But he had never said a thing before. Why not? US officials knew that Israel had been responsible for most of the ceasefire violations, but Reagan indicated otherwise in his press conference a few days before. Even the Israeli assault in West Beirut, in contemptuous disregard of Reagan's warning, drew only muffled criticism from the White House.

It took 'the air strikes and the Israeli advance into northern Lebanon' on 11 and 12 August, just when Habib's latest peace negotiations were 'at the point of success', to bring Reagan to state publicly 'what he [had] confirmed in private correspondence with . . . Begin — that United States support might be firm but it is not unconditional' (in an editorial from the *New York Times*, published in the IHT, 14–15 August).

Reagan's attitudes led him to adopt the wrong style with Begin.

> If President Reagan really wanted Israel to stop strangling West Beirut last week, how come he couldn't? Israel is wholly dependent on American military and economic aid. America is just about its only friend . . . Whatever interests drove them to Beirut, none is as vital as the link to the United States. So when Ron insists, why doesn't Menachem listen?
>
> One problem lies in those 'Dear Menachem' letters that 'Your friend, Ron,' kept sending. In Israeli politics, they have been like blank cheques, unwitting endorsements of the whole range of Begin policies . . . Even if Israelis judge America to be angry now, they think there is a wealth of understanding to be drawn down (*New York Times*, above).

Another problem in style was Reagan's sudden rages against Israeli bombing raids. Was Reagan's outrage sincere? 'Even while threatening Israel, he was reaffirming its demand that the PLO leave Lebanon.'

In another editorial the *New York Times* spoke of Reagan as moving 'from impatient scowls to vague threats to squeeze Israel' (published in the IHT, 6 August). On 2 August, at the very time when Israel was conducting what was then 'the heaviest Israeli shelling and bombing of the war', Reagan sent birthday greetings to Begin and 'also asked him "to please allow Mr Habib to conduct his negotiations in Beirut in an atmosphere conducive to their success".' ('Chronicle of a Bombardment' by Charles T. Powers, IHT, 3 August).

To Israelis, Reagan's letters criticising and endorsing their actions at the same time, and his sudden outbursts of rage at their bombing of Beirut, indicated a lack of seriousness of purpose, and severely crippled Washington's ability to deal with Begin.

He also took a vacation in California in the middle of the crisis, and at a time of uncertainty in Washington, just after Haig's resignation and before Shultz's confirmation. 'Though Habib files reports to Washington, observers on the spot believe that Habib has had no direct telephone conversations with President Reagan for several weeks now' (*The Times*, 30 July). As an editorial in *The Times* (24 August) said: Reagan's 'thinking has largely failed to connect with events'.

Although George Shultz took over as Secretary of State on a platform of 'peace and justice', it took him just over three weeks to obtain peace for Beirut. His personal qualities — dislike of confrontation (complementing the President's own) and a judicious, calm and controlled aura — did nothing to speed a negotiated settlement in Beirut. The predicted toughening of Washington towards Jerusalem just did not happen. Instead the emphasis was on continuity.

The administration continued with its trial-and-error method of trying to reach a settlement of the problem of Palestinian withdrawal — the US proposing and Israel disposing (of elements it did not like) by bombing Beirut. As under Haig, public US reaction to Israeli escalation remained low-key: 'When [after the bombings of early August] three members of Reagan's inner cabinet urged him to threaten sanctions, the President backed by his Secretary of State, George Shultz, declined. There was to be no strong confrontation with Begin, he said.' (the *Sunday Times*, 8 August).

The two instances on which the US imposed sanctions on Israel during the campaign were the suspension of deliveries of aircraft in mid-June and the indefinite suspension of deliveries of cluster-bombs in the third week of July. But because there was no plan for imposing sanctions they had no effect on the conduct of Israeli policy.

What Reagan could have done, but refused to entertain, was to withdraw a proposal he had made to Congress in May for the biggest-ever US arms transfer to Israel, worth $2.5 billion, and to recommend that Congress re-examine its intention of converting most of US aid to Israel from loans to gifts (see an editorial in the *Chicago Sun-Times*, 9 June).

By preserving the continuity of US policy on Lebanon, Reagan and Shultz only prolonged the crisis and the agony of Beirut. George Ball, a former US Under-Secretary of State, criticised the administration for failing to pressure both sides to make concessions. 'Instead of trying to exact any commitment from the Israelis, we foolishly concentrated solely on getting the PLO to leave. In other words, we pulled the Israelis' chestnuts out of the fire for nothing.' Ball argued that the US image in the world had suffered from association with the Israeli war effort (*Time*, 23 August).

There was a difference, however, between Shultz and Haig. Shultz 'has no emotional debts to the Jewish state', wrote Eric Silver (the *Observer*, 27 June). During his Senate confirmation hearings he would not be drawn into a discussion of the PLO's connection with 'international terrorism' and 'in one strikingly unequivocal sentence, he set out the core of his thinking: "The crisis in Lebanon makes painfully and totally clear a central reality of the Middle East: the legitimate needs and problems of the Palestinian people must be addressed and resolved — urgently and in all their dimensions".'

He stated that 'representatives of the Palestinians themselves must participate in the negotiating process', without allowing himself to be drawn on the difficult question of who, apart from the PLO, might fill the role. But he also said: 'People speak of the need for "tough talk" with Israel, but my approach, and my view of our best diplomatic shot, lies in emphasising the rewards of peace' (Peter Wilsher in the *Sunday Times*, 18 July).

It remains to be seen whether Shultz will make the necessary break with Haig's 'soft line' to achieve the justice for the Palestinians that peace in the Middle East region requires. Although Haig has gone, Washington still speaks of the 'opportunities' offered by the new situation in the area. Shultz's statements lead one, however, to believe that his 'opportunities' would be defined differently from Haig's.

Reagan's 'fresh start' announced on 1 September 1982, calling for 'full autonomy' for the Palestinians of the West Bank and Gaza in association with Jordan and a 'settlement freeze' by Israel in those areas, indicates that Shultz has had some success in pushing the administration towards a more even-handed policy. But unless he and Reagan are willing to both talk tough with Israel, and follow tough talk with tough action to coerce Israel into withdrawing from Lebanon and permitting Palestinian self-rule in the occupied territories, there will be no peace in the Middle East.

From the Silence of Arab Brothers . . .

On the morning after the invasion, the state-controlled Lebanese radio declared, 'Arab silence is stunning,' summing up what was to be a story of Arab inaction for the full eleven weeks of the Israeli military campaign in Lebanon.

Lebanese Foreign Minister Fuad Butros complained that the 'Arabs

appeared to be taking Israeli aggression against [Lebanon] for granted.'
(quoted in the *New York Times*, 7 June).

'The absence of an effective response by Arab nations to the Israeli
onslaught against the Palestinians in Lebanon is attributed by many Arabs
to their overwhelming sense of helplessness,' Thomas L. Friedman wrote
from Beirut (the *New York Times*, 21 June).

> 'The Israelis counted on the inter-Arab divisions when they launched
> their invasion,' an official of the [PLO] said. 'And they were right.'
> ... 'I don't understand how the Arabs can be so ineffectual when the
> Israelis are knocking at the gates of an Arab capital,' Yasser Arafat,
> the PLO chairman, said in a radio address last week. . . . The removal
> of Egypt from the ranks of the enemies of Israel and the disagreements
> over the Iran-Iraq war have left the Arabs too weak militarily and too
> divided politically to act in concert either regionally or internationally.
>
> The Arabs' military weakness is largely a result of the fact that two
> (Egypt and Iraq) of the three (with Syria) main Arab armies have been
> removed from the Arab-Israeli military equation . . . With Jordan not
> about to go to war . . . only Syria was left . . . Damascus played a very
> dangerous game with the Israelis, trying to protect as much of its area
> of control in Lebanon as possible without becoming embroiled in a full-
> scale one-to-one fight with Israel.

Anthony McDermott wrote of Jordan's 'sense of shock and humiliation
at Israel's invasion of Lebanon', which emphasised a 'mood of impotence
and vulnerability' in the country, where the invasion had been most 'acutely
felt'. King Hussein, a long-standing friend of the West, was 'known to be
extremely bitter about US attitudes' and at the ineffectual protests of the
EEC (*Financial Times*, 9 July).

When the Libyan leader Colonel Muammar Gaddafi sent a letter to Arafat
'suggesting ungenerously that the PLO leaders should commit suicide rather
than surrender to the Israelis', Arafat 'sent a sharp little note back . . .
reproaching him for "his tone of despair" and suggesting that if the colonel
had fulfilled all the pledges of support he had made to the PLO, then the
Palestinians might not be in their present predicament' (Robert Fisk, *The
Times*, 6 July). The Palestinians felt much the same way about all the Arab
leaders.

On Saturday, 17 July, the East Jerusalem newspaper *Al-Quds* summed up
what many people in the West Bank were feeling:

> 'The Arab peoples have been afflicted with blood-stained and hostile
> leaders whose only concern has been to hold on to power, while their
> peoples, sad and abandoned, look on . . . unable to do anything.'
> The Arabs were 'scattered and split in word and deed . . . divided as
> never before . . . Long ago the poet said: "The man who grazes his
> sheep in a wild land/And sleeps, will lose his flock to the lion".'

. . . To the Cold Comfort of the Soviet Union

At the end of the second week of the Israeli invasion of Lebanon, US
Secretary of State Haig 'described the Soviet attitude . . . as "encouragingly
cautious".' US officials believed that an agreement between Presidents
Reagan and Brezhnev to 'prevent the conflict from widening was vital for an
early ceasefire' (Anatole Kaletsky, *Financial Times*, 14 June).

Prevention of a widening of the conflict seemed to be the theme of Soviet
policy until the final ceasefire was imposed. Primarily the Soviet Union was
anxious to protect its investment in the Syrian regime of President Hafez
al-Assad, by preventing the Israelis from provoking the Syrian army into full-
scale hostilities. On 5 July, Soviet Foreign Minister Andrei Gromyko told the
Kuwaiti, Moroccan and PLO foreign ministers, in Moscow, that the Soviet
Union did not intend to get directly embroiled in the crisis, but would use
its influence 'behind the scenes', presumably with the US, to bring about an
Israeli withdrawal (the *Jerusalem Post*, 7 July).

Hella Pick reported on 9 July (*The Guardian*) that

> the Soviet Union has been forced into reluctant support of American
> management of the Beirut crisis, although it still hopes to extract some
> advantage for itself and the PLO. This emerged yesterday with the
> publication of a message from President Brezhnev to President Reagan
> in which the Russian leader called on the US to 'do its utmost' to end
> Israeli aggression in Lebanon. . . . It is possible to interpret [this]
> message as an indication that the Soviet Union now feels there is no
> alternative but to leave it to the US to extricate the PLO from their
> situation in Beirut, a course that would require at least de facto
> recognition of the PLO.

But when just this nearly happened in July the Israeli airforce stepped in
to prevent it from taking place by bombing West Beirut. Brezhnev's statement
also warned the US not to send troops to Beirut — this was seen as a
'rhetorical gesture designed for Arab consumption' — a warning which went
unheeded by Washington for, at the appointed time, American marines were
landed to help supervise the PLO evacuation.

If the Arab regimes lost credibility in the eyes of the Arab peoples, the
Americans and the Russians lost credibility in the eyes of the world.

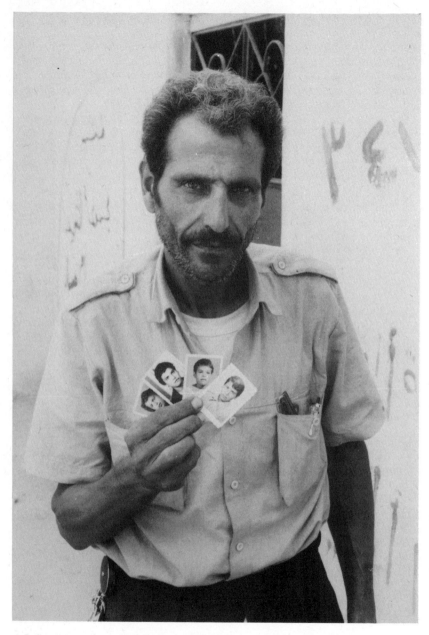

A Palestinian whose 4 children were killed in the massacre (Rex)

5. The Massacre

A Hollow Victory

After the ceasefire of 12 August the Israelis were vouchsafed only a fortnight, in Sharon's words, to 'enjoy their victory'. It did seem a victory of sorts because 13,000 Palestinian fighters and Syrian troops were evacuated from Beirut during that period: the first contingent went by ship to Larnaca in Cyprus on 21 August and Yasser Arafat sailed away to Greece on 30 August en route to Tunis; thus a substantial part of the PLO's armed forces, and its political and military leadership, was dispersed among eight Arab countries, as far apart as Iraq, South Yemen and Algeria.

It was, however, a qualified victory because each contingent was given an emotional and enthusiastic send-off from Beirut, with the troops bearing arms, smartly uniformed and flashing the V-for-victory sign. When they arrived at their new homes they were given a heroes' welcome and were greeted by the head of state. King Hussein was on hand to give his personal accolade to each of the fighters who were in the first batch to arrive in Jordan. Even the non-Arab Cypriots cheered those who passed through, and in Athens Arafat was given a full official, ceremonial welcome. 'We were not defeated' was the theme of the whole operation and, by and large, world opinion seemed to be in agreement with that message.

Though this defiant repudiation of the military fact was inexplicable and irritating to Israelis, they too benefited from the peace and quiet which prevailed in Beirut following the Habib agreement. With the departure of the Palestinians they were supposed to pull their troops back from the outskirts of Beirut to Khaldeh, south of the international airport. But there was no sign of any such move, and in fact Israeli military transport planes went on using the airport, which the Israelis renamed King Hiram Airport, to honour the Phoenician king who had helped Solomon to build the temple in Jerusalem.

Yet even during that fortnight the criticism of Israel because of its bombardment of the city became muted, and a correspondent of the *Jerusalem Post* (international edition, 5–11 September) reported that the American media were tilting back to their normal pro-Israeli stance. In that same issue another writer urged the Israelis not to give way to what he called 'unfounded guilt feelings about the death of innocent civilians', because the IDF had done 'everything possible to avoid spilling innocent blood'.

Then, on 1 September, two things happened, one publicly and one in secret, that were to cut short Israel's enjoyment of its victory.

The first was a nationally televised address by President Reagan in which he presented a comprehensive American peace plan to resolve the Arab-Israeli conflict. The President claimed that it was an even-handed proposal but, to judge by the reactions to it, it was very much less welcome to the Israelis than to the Arabs. Displaying unusual restraint and moderation, Arab and PLO spokesmen merely said that the plan contained some interesting ideas and could be a basis for discussion. Begin, on the other hand, described 1 September as 'the saddest day in his life' since he had become Prime Minister, and immediately rejected the plan outright.

On 2 September a unanimous Israeli Cabinet also rejected it, declaring that it would not even discuss the plan with anybody. The salient points of the Reagan plan were three. It rejected both a Palestinian state on the West Bank and Israeli sovereignty over that area, proposing instead Palestinian self-government in association with Jordan. It called for a halt to the setting up of new Jewish settlements and the enlarging of existing ones. And, perhaps most significantly, it declared that the future of Jerusalem would have to be decided after negotiations, thus implicitly rejecting Israel's annexation of Arab Jerusalem and the solemn, formal Knesset declaration that the Holy City was the unified and eternal capital of the Jewish State.

To make its rejection crystal clear the Israeli government promptly announced the establishment of eight new settlements in the occupied territories.

This hasty rejection of the plan, however, revived the Israeli Opposition's criticism of the Begin government's conduct of the war in Lebanon, and the Labour Party leader, Shimon Peres, stated that the American plan should be discussed. What was worse, the all-important Jewish community in the United States was also divided in its rejection. Many of its influential leaders took the same line as Peres and, as reported by Henry Brandon (*Sunday Times*, 12 September), 'no major Jewish organisation has rejected the President's proposals'. An Israeli was probably not far from the truth when he told the BBC correspondent in Jerusalem: 'We are being punished for what we did in Lebanon.'

Moreover, the hitherto divided Arabs, in a summit conference of heads of state at Fez, redeemed the collapse of the earlier meeting also at Fez, in November 1981, and unanimously agreed on an Arab peace plan, more or less incorporating the ideas originally put forward by Crown Prince Fahd, now King Fahd of Saudi Arabia. The plan gave strong backing to the PLO, called for an Israeli withdrawal to the 1967 borders and the establishment of a West Bank state, with Jerusalem as its capital, and, in an ambiguous phrase, gave 'implicit' recognition to Israel. Though this Arab plan differed significantly from Reagan's, it was not rejected by the Americans or by anybody else — except Israel, which dismissed it out of hand.

Shortly afterwards the Pope, despite furious protests from Israel, received Yasser Arafat in private audience in Rome, to express his sympathy for 'the sufferings of the Palestinian people'. Thus, by the end of the first fortnight of September, Israel, though it was no longer dropping bombs on Lebanon, was once again isolated and the target of universal criticism.

It had even lost the friendship of its Lebanese Maronite allies. This was the result of the second event to occur on 1 September. When, on 23 August, the Israelis helped Bechir Gemayel, commander of the Maronite militia, to be elected as president of Lebanon, the Israelis seemed to have achieved the major political objective of their invasion – the installation of a friendly, or dependent, regime which would sign a peace treaty with Israel. It all seemed so certain that Begin was the first foreign leader to send a fulsome message of congratulation to his 'dear friend' Bechir Gemayel.

But, quite soon, things began to go wrong. Under persistent questioning from Israeli reporters, Gemayel was notably reticent on the issue of a peace treaty. He had to be, if he genuinely wanted to be the president of all the Lebanese, including the Muslim majority which opposed peace with Israel. This seemed a poor return, however, for the $100 million in aid which, according to Begin, Israel had given to the Phalange since 1976.

So the President-elect of Lebanon was summoned to meet secretly with Begin, Sharon and Shamir (and perhaps Saad Haddad) somewhere in northern Israel. Opinion was divided on the wisdom of this move: 'Begin's expert advisers are said to have tried in vain to dissuade the prime minister from tackling the Lebanese president-elect on the matter at this juncture'. (*Jerusalem Post*, international edition, 5–11 September). But the tough Sharon line prevailed: the application of 'heavy Israeli pressure on Gemayel not to backtrack on commitments he allegedly made in the past to sign a peace treaty' (*Jerusalem Post*, international edition, 12–18 September).

After a four-hour discussion which went on into the small hours of the morning, Gemayel maintained his refusal to state publicly that, once he became president, he would sign a peace treaty. He later complained bitterly, as reported by Israel radio, that at the meeting he 'had been treated like a bell-boy'.

On Friday, 3 September, Sharon broke the news of the secret meeting, and when an embarrassed Gemayel angrily denied it, Sharon released convincing details of it – all of which, according to Asher Wallfish (*Jerusalem Post*, international edition, 5–11 September) made Begin 'furious'.

The result was that Gemayel distanced himself even further from the Israelis through repeated calls for the withdrawal of all foreign forces from Lebanon. In a much publicised meeting of reconciliation with the veteran Lebanese Muslim leader Saeb Salam, Gemayel declared it would be up to the Lebanese Parliament to decide whether Lebanon should make peace with Israel – and that was hardly likely.

Gemayel even sent a message to King Fahd in which he suggested that, when the king sent him the routine message of congratulation after his formal inauguration, he should express the wish that Lebanon remain a member of the Arab family – in other words, no separate peace with Israel – and that all foreign forces should withdraw.

It was noticeable that, in the first two weeks of September, Sharon went out of his way to declare that, if there was not to be a peace treaty with Israel, Israel would make its own arrangements within a 'special security zone' 40 to 50 kilometres wide in southern Lebanon – but not necessarily through the presence of the Israeli army, thus implying Israel would use the Haddad militia. Sharon had particular words of praise for Haddad. As explained by Wallfish (*Jerusalem Post*, international edition, 12–18 September):

> The declarations of Israeli support for Haddad are not only intended to secure a role for him in supervising security affairs in the south . . . Israel could never expect such allies to come forward in the future if it let Haddad down now.

The Israelis had started the game of playing off one client against another, an easy game in the circumstances, because the Lebanese nationalist Phalange had consistently criticised Haddad's desertion from the Lebanese army.

Against this background of increasingly uneasy Phalangist-Israeli relations, Gemayel was suddenly assassinated by a massive bomb explosion at the Phalangist headquarters on Tuesday, 14 September. It was immediately assumed by Muslim and Christian Lebanese alike that the attack was the work of Israel. For many, Gemayel became a national hero who had paid with his life for standing up against the latest foreign occupier. An Israel Radio correspondent, Jack Katzenell, reported on 25 September that 99 per cent of the Christians he questioned in East Beirut believed that Israel was responsible for the killing.

The striking fact is that the Phalangist radio and newspapers did not accuse any of Bechir Gemayel's political enemies – the Syrians, the Palestinians or the leftist Muslims – of the crime. Curiously, they accused no one; perhaps because they could hardly accuse Israel publicly, perhaps because it was immediately obvious that the bombing could only have been an inside job by a Phalangist with free access to the heavily-guarded Phalangist headquarters.

James MacManus of the *Guardian* reported on 18 September the Maronite

> suspicion that their own co-religionists may have had a hand in the murder. . . . The precision required to mount the attack points to a professional conspiracy which almost certainly must have involved Phalangist dissidents.

It was recalled that, even during the civil war, Bechir had had trouble with a strongly pro-Israeli faction within the Phalange which Israel had succeeded in building up from cadres trained in Israel. Such men would not have approved of Bechir's refusal to commit himself to a peace treaty. It is known that the Phalangist security force arrested hundreds of Phalangist members after the explosion.

Robert Fisk (*The Times*, 16 September) made this tart comment on
Gemayel's assassination:

> Israel's critics will not be slow to point out how dangerous it is for Arab
> leaders to grasp Mr Begin's hand of friendship. Bechir Gemayel died
> almost exactly a year after the assassination of Mr Sadat.

The Lebanese drew the opposite conclusion — how dangerous it was to lose
the friendship of Begin and of Israel's local allies.

Israel Occupies West Beirut

As soon as it was known that Gemayel had indeed been killed in the explosion
(and the Israeli authorities had the news three or four hours before the
official announcement was made) Begin and Sharon conferred by telephone
and, without any Cabinet consultation, decided to move the Israeli army into
West Beirut. When the advance began, on the morning of Wednesday the 15th,
the official reason was that it was 'to prevent dangerous developments' and
'to preserve tranquillity and order' — the implication being that there was a
danger the Phalangist militia might storm into Muslim West Beirut to take
revenge for Gemayel's murder, presumably by the Muslims. But Beirut was
quiet on Tuesday night, because it was obvious to Beirutis that no Muslim
could have carried out the murder.

At about midday on Wednesday, the US envoy Morris Draper was given
the official Israeli explanation in Jerusalem, and the assurance that the Israeli
advance would be 'limited and precautionary': the Israel army, that is, would
not move into the whole of West Beirut but would only move as far north as
the Corniche Mazraa, the southern boundary of West Beirut proper. Because
Draper raised no objections, the Israelis later claimed that the US had been
consulted and had approved the move into West Beirut.

But even as Draper was being given assurances, the Israelis were crossing
the Corniche Mazraa and thrusting into the heart of West Beirut from the
east, south and west. By midday on Thursday the 16th, they had occupied
the whole city — the first Arab capital to fall to the Israeli invader.

The same day, the White House and the State Department, realising they
had been tricked by Israel, issued a demand for Israel's withdrawal from West
Beirut. The deception had been double. The first was the assurance given to
Draper. The second involved Israel's violation of the Habib agreement of 20
August. A State Department spokesman explained that this agreement had
been reached

> in the context of numerous oral assurances we had from Israel that it
> would not enter West Beirut. . . . At one point we debated whether it
> was necessary to obtain written Israeli assurances that the IDF would
> not enter West Beirut, but decided this was not necessary in light of

the many previous oral assurances we had obtained.

The US position was confused by a statement by President Reagan that 'what led them [the Israelis] to move in was an attack by some leftist militia forces there'. There was no such attack.

In fact the Israeli occupation of West Beirut was a military walk-over because the militias had been taken by surprise; they, too, had believed the Israeli assurances passed on to them by Habib. In the preceding two weeks they had removed the many barricades and bunkers that had blocked off the southern approaches to the city. They had stopped patrolling, and most of their defensive positions had been left unmanned. The Israeli tanks and armoured personnel carriers had a clear run. There was little that the hurriedly reorganised and lightly-armed militiamen could do.

Nevertheless 88 civilians were killed and 254 wounded during the three days it took the Israelis to occupy the city; the IDF suffered eight dead. In this inglorious feat of arms it was only through surprise and deception that the Israeli army was finally able to accomplish what, for the most part, it had not dared to attempt against the PLO defenders of Beirut. And the Israeli attack was rendered comically unheroic by the fact that when their soldiers advanced down a street, crouching under the weight of their arms and flak-jackets, TV camera crews moved backwards ahead of them.

Yet neither the Americans not the militias should have been taken by surprise, because the Israelis had prepared the ground, militarily and politically, for their eventual advance. On 3 September, in their first violation of the Habib agreement, and in line with their tactic of 'improving positions', they had pushed troops forward to a ridge overlooking the Sabra-Chatila refugee camp. This, they said, was to clear mines, which they did; but by doing so they opened up a main axis of advance.

The Israelis were also loud in their protestations that the PLO had broken the Habib agreement by handing over some of its heavy arms to the militias and leaving behind 2,000 fighters in Beirut. That figure was repeated many times and was built up into a myth comparable, on a minor scale, to the myth of the armouries for a million men allegedly unearthed in south Lebanon.

After the full horror of the massacre that followed in the Sabra-Chatila camp had made a mockery of the original Israeli claim that the IDF was sent into Beirut to stop bloodshed, Sharon finally decided to tell the truth, or a version of it. On 24 September, during a television programme in Israel, he confessed that the original justification had been 'camouflage' and that the 'real' reason was to eliminate the '2,000 terrorists'.

But what happened to these '2,000 terrorists'? If there had been that number of fighters, heavily armed and left behind in Beirut, there would have been a real battle for the city and the killer squads in Sabra-Chatila would have met with determined armed resistance — whereas, in fact, there was almost none. In all the many accounts of the pogrom there was no Israeli claim that hundreds, let alone thousands, of 'terrorists' were captured or eliminated. So either Israeli intelligence had genuinely got its figures wrong, or it had greatly exaggerated them.

Or perhaps there was another reason altogether for the move into Beirut. Perhaps it was a question of psychology, of Sharon's psychology. For ten weeks the full might of the Israeli army, airforce and navy had been held at bay by the PLO defenders whom the Israelis had not dared to attack on the ground, and by the people of Beirut who had rejected the Israeli invitation to run away. That prolonged and successful defiance was bad for the morale and reputation of the Israeli armed forces, and equally for Sharon's image as a forceful, thrusting commander.

So West Beirut had to come under Israeli dominance and if that had to be achieved by strategem rather than by assault, Sharon could still say, as he eventually told an army audience, 'in the end we did it'.

There could be yet another reason for the Israeli occupation of Beirut, however. It must be asked whether the massacre was simply an unfortunate result of the Israeli occupation, or whether it was, conceivably, one of its causes. In other words, did the Israeli army go into Beirut in order to inflict on the Palestinians the terror and shock that the killings were all-too-successful in bringing about? An examination of what actually happened in the Sabra-Chatila camps may provide us with the answer. A great deal has been written about this horrible event. What follows is a compilation from many accounts, notably from detailed studies published in *Time* magazine (27 September and 4 October), *The Times* (20 and 24 September) and the *Sunday Times* (26 September).

The Massacre

First, the setting. The Sabra-Chatila area is a rather narrow rectangle, between a quarter and half a mile from east to west, and perhaps a mile and a half from north to south; Sabra is the northern end, Chatila the southern. Chatila is a UN-administered camp for Palestinians who had been driven into Lebanon in 1948–50, most of them from northern Palestine. The site was probably chosen because, at the Chatila end, there is a stand of umbrella pines which provided shade; the pines, rather bedraggled, are still there.

The word 'camp' has become a misnomer because the original tents and lean-tos have been replaced by small one-room or two-room structures made of cement blocks with corrugated iron roofs held down by large stones. There are also quite a few other larger two-storey structures and shops, workshops, schools, clinics and a large hospital. Most of these buildings were sited haphazardly so there is no pattern of roads, only a confusion of dusty, or in winter slushy, unpaved alleyways.

So while it is a bit better than a bidonville, it is not much more than a sprawling, sleazy suburb of Beirut. The water and electricity provided to the Chatila camp by UNRWA attracted other poor folk — southern Shias looking for work in Beirut, Kurds, Syrian labourers — who settled round the edges of the camp, so that it expanded southwards to meet the airport road and north-

Victims of the Sabra Massacre (Rex)

wards to the equally poor district of Sabra. Further north again, Sabra met the lower-middle-class Fakhani area, where the Arab University and PLO headquarters were located.

With this expansion the population of the combined Sabra-Chatila area ceased to be wholly, or even mainly, Palestinian: the core population of Chatila, the 5,000-odd registered Palestinian refugees, grew to perhaps 20,000 persons. But, however mixed the population, the area became and remained a Palestinian stronghold, with underground shelters and storage depots and, especially after the civil war, high earthworks thrown up on some of its outer limits.

When, at dawn on Wednesday the 15th, the Israeli army moved into West Beirut, two of its prongs moved past Sabra-Chatila. One passed to the west of the camp, from an assembly point near the Kuwait Embassy, northwards past the sports stadium. The other passed to the east, along the road that is the continuation of the boulevard to the airport. When the Israelis, at midday, captured the buildings of the Arab University, just north of Sabra, the area was completely surrounded. Indeed that evening General Eitan announced that all four Palestinian camps in the Beirut area were surrounded, cut off and 'hermetically sealed': at the time it was assumed that this was to protect them.

On Thursday the 16th, Israeli troops and armour around the camps were, at the furthest, 300 yards away and, at the nearest, 50 yards from the boundaries. So when the Christian militiamen, who did the killing, went into Sabra-Chatila, they could only do so with the permission of the Israelis.

Indeed, according to *Time* magazine (4 October),

> Top Israeli officers planned many months ago to enlist the Lebanese Forces, made up of the combined Christian militias headed by Bechir Gemayel, to enter the Palestinian refugee camps once an Israeli encircle-ment of West Beirut had been completed.

Colin Campbell (*New York Times*, 1 October) said that:

> The plan for Christian militiamen to enter the camps had been discussed for some time between Israeli and Christian officers — that it had been outlined in fact before the assassination of Bechir Gemayel.

The *Sunday Times* (26 September) gave the work-name for this 'carefully pre-planned military operation' to 'purge' the camps as *Moah Barzel*, or Iron Brain; the contents, it said, 'were already largely familiar to Sharon and Begin'; Moah Barzel was part of Sharon's larger plan to assault West Beirut which had been discussed and turned down by the Israeli Cabinet on 17 July.

Time magazine is more specific: 'By Sharon's own admission the Israelis planned two weeks ago to have the Lebanese Forces enter the camps.' Thus if the plan was known months or weeks ahead to the political and military leaders of Israel, it was known equally to the political and military leadership of the Phalange.

As *Time* (4 October) put it:

> On several occasions Gemayel told Israeli officials he would like to raze the camps and flatten them into tennis courts. Gemayel's offer of support fitted in well with Israeli thinking. . . . Gemayel had initially planned to use his troops in West Beirut; earlier this year he had sent 500 of them to Israel for special training. . . . The Christian militia forces that were known to have gone into the camps, according to both Israeli and Lebanese sources, had been trained by the Israelis.

Campbell (*New York Times*, 1 October) states that Sharon and Gemayel had met several times in the weeks before 15 September, and that a Lebanese army officer had said that 'originally the Christians were to have occupied the camps on 24 September. The plan, he said, may have been speeded up after the assassination'. The 24th would have been the day after Gemayel's inauguration as president — hardly an auspicious beginning.

If it is asked why such a high-level, carefully planned action against the camps was deemed necessary, the simple answer is: Ain Hilweh. The Israelis believed that they had to 'purge' Sabra-Chatila; but they could not repeat the tactics used at Ain Hilweh. They could not bring down on Sabra-Chatila the sort of massive bombardment that had reduced Ain Hilweh to rubble — not after Reagan's angry order to stop such bombardments in West Beirut. If troops went in without a prior softening up, they feared they would suffer even higher casualties than those at Ain Hilweh.

So the Israelis chose to use the Christian militia which was able, ready, and willing to do the job. In the days after the massacre, Sharon said repeatedly that the Phalangists were used so as to avoid Israeli casualties.

But was the Israeli assumption correct, that there were large numbers of 'terrorists' in the camps? Clearly not. Robert Suro (*Time*, 4 October) reported, after visiting Sabra-Chatila in the days before the attack, that there was no military presence there:

> There thus appeared to be no need for the Israelis to have sent a strong armed force into the camps to search them thoroughly, much less a Christian force that might want to wreak vengeance on Palestinian civilians. . . . The Israelis fell victim to their obsession with the supposed presence of the PLO in West Beirut.

So the most tragic aspect of this massacre is that it was all a mistake; it was unnecessary.

After Begin and Sharon decided, late on Tuesday the 14th, to go ahead with Operation Iron Brain, its actual implementation began the next day. According to Campbell (*New York Times*, 1 October)

> Sharon suggested in a recent statement to parliament that the plan [for

entering the camp] was worked out on Wednesday, 15 September . . . shortly after Israeli troops began moving into West Beirut. . . . . Sharon told the Knesset that the general staff and commander-in-chief of the Phalangists met twice with Israel's ranking generals on 15 September and discussed entering the camps, which they did the next afternoon.

Most journalistic accounts mistakenly say that these meetings took place on Thursday, but this would not have left enough time for the Phalangists to assemble their forces. Those present at the meetings were, on the Israeli side, Major-General Amir Drori, head of Northern Command, Brigadier Amos Yaron, divisional commander for West Beirut, and perhaps two other senior officers. The Phalangists were represented by their commander-in-chief, Fadi Ephraim, and Elias Hobeika, 'the intelligence chief, who had attended the Staff and Command College in Israel. He was to be the main leader of the groups that went into the camps' (*Time*, 4 October).

According to Campbell, Sharon stated that General Eitan also attended both the Wednesday meetings. Campbell also asserts that all the top leaders of the Phalangist militia were involved, including Dib Anastas, head of military police, and Joseph Edde, commander of the militia forces in southern Lebanon.

Complete official Israeli confirmation of this planning stage was provided by Colonel Yehuda Levy, the IDF spokesman in Beirut, who said (*Sunday Times*, 26 September) that the Phalange forces

> were briefed on Wednesday and then again, just before they stormed the camps, in the course of Thursday. 'We have troop commanders in the field and they briefed and co-ordinated the Lebanese Forces,' said Levy last week. . . . They were told to take as many leftist and PLO prisoners as possible, to clear the area and to let the civilians get back to normal.

Because of all this high-level Israeli-Phalangist planning and co-ordination, it is certain that most of the troops involved in the massacre were regular members of the Phalangist militia and indeed of a well-trained elite unit. At first it was thought that most of the killers came from Haddad's militia. People in the camps themselves said so, but this does not seem to be correct; Haddad himself has said that the story was concocted by his 'Christian enemies in Beirut' and he has welcomed an inquiry. Perhaps 40–50 Haddad men were involved, with probably a few score from what had once been the 'Tiger' force of Camille Chamoun's militia.

Earlier suppositions that the Phalangists were dissident members of the militia can no longer be entertained. Does one therefore have to believe that the new leader of the Phalange Party, Amin Gemayel, knew nothing of what his militia leaders and their men were doing? Probably not; he had just taken over amidst considerable confusion, his dead brother had yet to be buried and he had never had very close connections with the militia. So, taking advantage of the confusion, the militia seems to have acted on its own to implement a plan worked out with the Israelis well in advance.

Between 1,000 and 1,200 militiamen seem to have been involved, with about half of them actually in the area at any one time. It is possible that many of the militiamen came from what has been called the Damour Battalion, whose members could be relied upon to be particularly vengeful.

Because vengeance is long-lasting in Lebanon, the story goes back six and a half years, to February 1976. In that month the Phalangists attacked and overran the slummy Qarantina area from which the Palestinians and Shias had prevented access to Beirut port. A massacre followed.

The survivors of the Qarantina massacre fled to Sabra-Chatila and to nearby beach clubs. In that same month the Maronite inhabitants of Damour, a village on the coastal highway south of Beirut, emboldened by the presence of former President Chamoun and some members of his Tiger militia in his villa at nearby Sadiyat, decided to close the coastal road; this was the eleventh month of the civil war and no harm had come to the people of Damour, who had till then kept quiet.

This act of provocation, by closing the highway, cut southern Lebanon in two and could not be tolerated by the Palestinians and Lebanese leftists, who got their food and fuel from the south. They stormed Damour, killed many of its people and drove the rest into the grounds of Chamoun's villa from where, under the auspices of Yasser Arafat himself, they were evacuated by sea to the Maronite area north of Beirut. To underline this point, many of the Qarantina people were moved into Damour.

On the day after the Israelis overran Damour, they invited its former inhabitants to return, and, even though the village had been badly damaged, many did so. Certainly, on the afternoon of Thursday, 16 September, local residents observed large groups of militia, in trucks and jeeps, moving up from the south, from the direction of Damour, towards an assembly point at Beirut international airport which was an IDF command post and supply depot.

It was here that a Phalangist officer explained to an Israel Radio reporter, with the help of an Israel airforce aerial photograph, that his men were going into the camps and that 'the aim of the operation is to kill the terrorists'; this report was broadcast on Thursday the 16th. At about 3 pm they were seen moving out of the airport in a convoy, with Israeli armoured cars and tanks. Pictures of this convoy, moving past Israeli checkpoints, were taken by an Israeli cameraman and shown on Israeli television on the night of Saturday the 18th. The militiamen even assembled in a building opposite the Kuwaiti Embassy that became their headquarters, and between 5 pm and 6 pm they entered Chatila from the south-west and began their killing.

The killing went on, intermittently, for the next 40 hours, until about 10 am on Saturday the 18th. So much has been written about that grim and horrible happening that it is not necessary to repeat the details here. The pictures speak for themselves. All that needs to be said is that the victims were men, women and children, of all ages, from the very old to the very

young, even babes in arms. They were killed in every possible way. The lucky
ones were shot, singly or in groups. Others were strangled or had their throats
slit.

They were mutilated, before or after death; genitals and breasts were sliced
off; some had crosses carved on their chests, a Phalangist trademark. In the
hospitals, doctors, nurses and patients in their beds were killed, as witnessed
by foreign doctors. Some were buried alive, some dead, under the rubble of
their bulldozed homes, and many were dumped into hastily-dug mass graves.

What is necessary is to establish, once and for all, the responsibility for the
crime. One can be certain that this will, eventually, be done with thoroughness
and justice by the commission of inquiry set up, reluctantly, by the Begin
government. One is less certain that it will be done by the commission of
inquiry set up by the Lebanese government.

At 10.12 pm on Thursday the 16th, the IDF Radio, monitored by the
BBC, openly accepted a large degree of responsibility when it said:

> The intention is that the IDF will not operate tonight to purge the areas
> of Sabra and Chatila and nearby camps. It was decided to entrust the
> Phalangists with the mission of carrying out these purging operations.

At that time, at a meeting of the Israeli Cabinet, Begin was fighting a hard,
angry battle to win retrospective approval for the move into West Beirut. The
opposition group, led by deputy prime minister David Levy, called for an
immediate decision to withdraw. One minister described the whole affair as
'a scandal'.

That was only the beginning of the denunciations. But the Cabinet finally
approved the move, including the Phalangist entry into Sabra-Chatila (*Sunday
Times*, 26 September; the *Guardian* and *Financial Times*, 21 September).
It would not have done so if it had been aware of a message received at 11.10
pm at army headquarters in Tel-Aviv from Northern Command Headquarters
in Beirut. This quoted the Phalange commander in Chatila as reporting that
'until now 300 terrorists and civilians have been killed'. This message was
circulated to 20 officers but, somehow, General Eitan, it is officially stated,
did not receive his copy (*Sunday Times*, 26 September).

All through the night of Thursday, through Friday, Friday night and
Saturday morning, the Israeli units surrounding the Sabra-Chatila area were
co-operating fully with the Phalangist squads inside by firing hundreds of
flares into the night sky to illuminate the scene and enable the Phalangists
to continue their task after nightfall.

It has been argued that the IDF thought it was co-operating with the
Phalangists merely in rounding up 'terrorists', as they had been briefed to do.
If so, why has the IDF not reported on the seizure of all these 'terrorists'
who were supposed to have been in the camps? No 'terrorists' were brought
out alive, for the Phalangists said that they took no prisoners (Robert Suro,
Time, 27 September).

The Israeli army around the camps could not have been ignorant of what

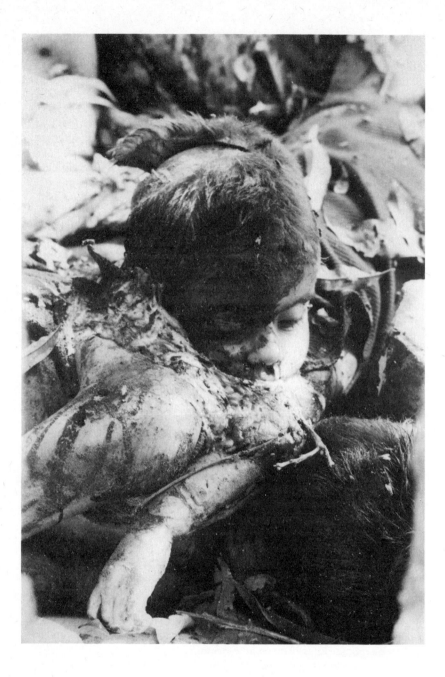

Victim of the Chatila Massacre (Rex)

was going on inside, and there is evidence that even on Thursday evening some soldiers knew. *Ha'aretz* (23 September) reported that, on Thursday evening, two soldiers reportedly told their officers that they suspected people were being massacred but were told, 'It's all right, don't worry.' The soldiers told a *Ha'aretz* reporter that crying women ran out of Chatila and spread the news: an Israeli officer said their flight had been dismissed as hysteria.

Robert Fisk (*The Times*, 25 September) reported that a Lebanese army officer at a nearby barracks told him 'on Thursday night hundreds of women and children and old men came to me here — 500 of them — and pleaded with me to shelter them from Lebanese elements who were killing people at the camp'.

However cold-blooded or indifferent the soldiers on the spot may have been (and some were not), by 11.10 on that Thursday night Northern Command Headquarters knew that hundreds of civilians had already been killed, and so did Israeli army headquarters back home.

Even more people got to know what was happening on Friday morning, including non-military people in Tel-Aviv. At 11 am the Communications Minister, Mordechai Zipori, received a call from Ze'ev Schiff, Israel's most respected defence correspondent, that stories were coming out of a massacre in Chatila. Zipori told Foreign Minister Shamir, but Shamir later said he could get no information from the army.

As to the army in Beirut itself, General Drori, in an interview with Tom Friedman (*New York Times*, 28 September) said that, on Friday morning, he and Brigadier Yaron had 'an uncomfortable feeling' that the Phalangists were doing something wrong. Drori said that, at the time, neither knew about the message of 11.10 pm Thursday, that about 300 people had already been killed — even though the report went out from Drori's own Northern Command headquarters. This, he said, was 'an item that was being checked. . . . But he said that after he and . . . Eitan met with the Phalangists at 4.30 that afternoon, they were allowed to continue this operation until Saturday morning.'

Journalists kept outside the camps heard the sounds of these 'operations' during Friday. Robert Suro (*Time*, 24 September) said that 'it was clearly not a firefight because the volleys of gunfire were not being returned: the guns were being fired in only one direction'. And 'an Israeli colonel in the vicinity said his troops would not interfere in what was going on, but declared that the area should be "purified" ' (*Monday Morning*, Beirut, 27 September).

How was it that throughout Friday, while the killing was going on, news of it did not leak out through the many correspondents who had begun to have their own 'uncomfortable feelings' around midday? The explanation is simple: after some of the camp residents had managed to flee on Thursday night, the Phalange force and the Israelis did not allow anyone out — or any correspondents in. Thus (*Time*, 4 October):

> On Friday afternoon a group of at least 400 people seeking refuge in **downtown West Beirut and carrying** a white flag approached Israeli

soldiers. The civilians said a massacre was taking place; they were turned back to the camps at gunpoint.

Loren Jenkens of the *Washington Post* and Robert Suro of *Time* were among correspondents ordered away on Friday afternoon and evening by Phalangists and Israelis; some photographers had their films ripped out of their cameras.

So the killings continued throughout Friday, Friday night and the morning of Saturday the 18th. When the militiamen finally left and the correspondents were able to go into Sabra-Chatila, at about 11 am, they found freshly bleeding corpses (Robert Fisk, *The Times*, 20 September).

The exact number of dead will never be known. It was decided not to open up some of the mass graves in the camps. Some bodies were still buried under the rubble of bulldozed houses. There were reports of truckloads of bodies being driven away, and there was an Egyptian report that the bodies of Egyptians killed in the massacre, perhaps over 50, were stuffed into helicopters and dropped into the sea.

At a rough estimate, perhaps a thousand people in all were slaughtered in Sabra-Chatila. But over 900 other people, mostly women and children, are known to have been put onto trucks and driven away; nothing has been heard of them since. Since Lebanon is a small country, their mass graves may eventually be found. If so, 2,000 people may have perished.

Most of them were civilians, not 'terrorists', and according to UNRWA 70 to 75 per cent were Lebanese. Thus an operation aimed at capturing 2,000 Palestinian 'terrorists' ended in the murder of 2,000 people, most of whom were neither terrorists nor Palestinians.

Sharon, after finally admitting that the Israeli army had sent the Phalangists into the camps, said, as a final defence, that no one could have imagined that the Phalangists would commit a massacre. But the *Washington Post* (1 October), in a report from its Jerusalem correspondent, said that in a meeting with Israeli officials, before the final decision was taken, Sharon had spoken of his 'worry' that a massacre could take place. He could not have been altogether ignorant of the sort of men he was sending in 'to arrest terrorists'.

Now that the main facts are known, it is instructive to look back at the Israeli attempts to cover up the truth. Up until the afternoon of Saturday the 18th, the Israeli government went on saying that it knew nothing of what had happened from Thursday night on — that its information had all come from the media. (Begin still holds to this story: must we then believe that the two men most responsible, the Israeli Prime Minister and the head of the Phalange Party, were both ignorant of what their men had done?)

On Sunday the 19th, it was said that, on Friday morning, Israeli troops had 'taken steps' to stop the killing, 'two hours after it began'. The Israeli spokesmen first refused to give details of what those steps were; then said that the Phalangists had been sent away from the area once they came out of the camps, also supposedly on Friday.

Spokesmen also said, variously, on Saturday and Sunday, that the IDF had prior knowledge of the 'purge', and possibly even co-operated with the Christian militia, but had no information on what the militiamen were doing in the camps; that the army had no prior knowledge because it was 'possible' the Phalange had gone in on their own, forcing their way past lightly-held Israeli positions; that the Christians had sneaked in, from the eastern side (Eitan said this); that they had broken in; and even that it was really the Lebanese army that had been in the camps.

Unfortunate or Premeditated?

Having reviewed what happened we can attempt to answer that earlier question: was the Sabra-Chatila massacre simply an unfortunate result of the Israeli occupation of Beirut, or was it pre-planned?

The evidence for a premeditated move is considerable. Operation Iron Brain, covering the move into Beirut and the camps, was prepared well in advance. We know that there had been consultation between the Israelis and Phalangists weeks, even months, ahead. And we now have information, from an Israeli source, that the Phalangists had been doing their own advance planning for an attack on Sabra-Chatila.

The independent and prestigious daily *Ha'aretz* reported on 28 September that, according to

> the conclusions of an enquiry by the Israeli intelligence service, the massacre was not the result of an explosion of anger and a desire for vengeance by the Phalangists, as claimed by the Israeli authorities.

The newspaper speaks of information pointing to

> a long-term objective studied over several weeks by the Phalangist leaders and aiming at the expulsion of the whole Palestinian population of Lebanon, beginning with Beirut. [The aim was] to create panic, to provoke an exodus, en masse, of Palestinians towards Syria and to convince all the Palestinians in Lebanon that they were no longer safe in that country.

It is significant that, as we have seen, Israeli and Phalangist officers met to discuss the Sabra-Chatila operation within hours of the Israelis moving into West Beirut, and that the fairly sizeable operation, for which the Phalangists had been provided with Israeli aerial photographs, began the very next day — hardly something that could have been done on the spur of the moment. For the Phalangists to undertake the operation on their own would have been too blatant: the presence of the Israeli army was necessary to provide security and cover, and to prevent victims from escaping from the area.

There was, to Arab minds, a precedent. David Shipler said in the *New York*

Times on 27 September:

> It was Mr Begin himself who recalled Deir Yassin. He brought it up at a
> cabinet meeting and in several private conversations. The name is a
> codeword of terror and anger and revenge among the Arabs, and a
> stain that has marked Mr Begin throughout most of his life.

On the night of 9–10 April 1948, gunmen of the Irgun Zvai Leumi underground movement, the head of which was Menachem Begin, attacked the
village of Deir Yassin that commanded the road to Jerusalem. Most of the
men of the village were away; 254 inhabitants, mostly old men, women and
children, were lined up and killed in cold blood and their bodies dumped in a
well.

> It all came back to him [Begin] last week. He was not in Deir Yassin
> himself, he pointed out, and knew nothing of it until after the fact.

Besides that disclaimer of Begin's there are other resemblances between
the two massacres: regular troops held the area (Haganah in 1948 and Israel's
army in 1982), while irregulars (the Irgun and the Phalange) went in to do the
slaughter; and in both cases the irregulars acted according to a plan co-ordinated
with the regulars.

In his biography, Begin refers to the 'victory' of Deir Yassin because it
panicked the Palestinians throughout the country into precipitate flight.
Sabra-Chatila seems to have had the same result. Its inhabitants fled the camp
and were so traumatised that it would take little more to get them out of
Lebanon altogether, as envisaged in the Phalangist plan revealed by *Ha'aretz*.
Such an exodus would also be welcome to the Israelis, who have openly
proclaimed that they do not wish the refugee camps to be reconstituted.

In the eyes of Israeli intelligence, the occupation of West Beirut was
probably fairly successful. The IDF certainly carted away quantities of files
and documents from the various PLO offices they ransacked. More important,
the Israelis gained information about the PLO's finances when, breaking
Lebanon's law on banking secrecy, they insisted on removing information
about PLO accounts in Beirut banks.

The PLO Research Centre was another target. It was emptied, including
its entire library of 10,000 volumes, manuscripts and archives. As the
director said later, 'They have plundered our Palestinian cultural heritage . . .
the papers we have lost are invaluable and possibly irreplaceable.' They made
up the world's largest collection of manuscripts on Palestine.

The Israelis also seized large quantities of arms and arrested several
hundred young men, Palestinians and Lebanese, some of whom had been
fighters in the ranks of the PLO groups and of the leftist and nationalist
Lebanese forces. But no irreparable damage was done to the anti-Israeli
forces in West Beirut.

At the end of the two-week occupation West Beirut was glad to see the back of the Israeli army, which left the city with a much lower reputation than when it came in. For one thing the Israelis, however heavily armed, simply failed to impose discipline on the normally anarchic Beirutis. Commands were defied, roadblocks cheerfully ignored; the Israeli army came up against the Lebanese chauffeur and lost. For another thing, the Israelis themselves were undisciplined and indulged in looting, mainly of small valuables but also of cars which were loaded onto tank transporters.

Above all, what disgusted the West Beirutis was the fact that the Israelis vandalised the apartments they moved into, smashing up what they could not carry away.

The Israelis seemed surprised, even hurt, that the people of West Beirut did not greet them as liberators, as had been the case in East Beirut. Cold hostility developed into violent hostility. As Robert Fisk reported (*The Times*, 27 September):

> The Israelis probably left the Muslim sector of the city just in time. By Saturday night, assassination attempts were being made against Israeli troops in West Beirut on an average of one every five hours and Israeli soldiers were fast becoming involved in a traditional guerrilla war.

Without the occupation of West Beirut there would have been no Sabra-Chatila massacre. The wave of condemnation that swept down on the Begin government after the massacre showed that the occupation was not just a failure, but a hideous mistake.

6. Ingesting Lebanon

The Army Stays

Israel's army likes to move fast and so do its politicians, especially when it comes to organising territory under occupation. As we have seen, both Defence Minister Sharon and Minister for Science Yuval Ne'eman had stated that they expected the Israeli army to stay in Lebanon, particularly south Lebanon, for a long while.

Hence it came as no surprise when, on 9 July, a month before the 'final' ceasefire, the Deputy Chief-of-Staff informed military correspondents that it was possible that the army would stay in Lebanon for the winter, and that preparations were being made accordingly. Tents would be replaced by prefabricated huts and, because of the winter rains, barrack sites would be moved to higher ground. Stoves and winter kit, including ski clothes, were being obtained; and all-weather roads, essential to an army of occupation, would be laid down. The coastal road in particular was widened, with the citrus groves and banana plantations bordering the old road being ruthlessly bulldozed away. A wide, brand-new, hard-topped highway pushed its way up the centre of the Bekaa Valley at the rate of a mile a day.

Indeed one of the first pieces of evidence that the Israeli occupation was going to last was the appearance, soon after the front line had moved forward, of regular, painted, metal road signs with the words in Hebrew above and Arabic below.

Even before the fighting stopped in Tyre and Sidon, and while the battle of Ain Hilweh was still going on and pockets of guerrillas were still holding out in the town, leaflets were dropped asking the people to go to the local administrative headquarters to obtain new identification papers and passes to move in and out of town.

Several correspondents reported long queues of people waiting for these papers and their complaints at the delays. Christopher Walker (*The Times*, 1 July) and Robert Fisk (*The Times*, 19 June) said that the papers were in Hebrew and carried the Star of David; Walker wrote of 'the military bureaucracy which now has everyone − Arab and Jew alike − in occupied Lebanon in its grip'.

This is a curious situation. Technically, Israel is not at war with Lebanon.

The Lebanese army did not fight the advancing Israeli army, and the structure of the Lebanese civil administration, exiguous at best and now pretty battered, is still in place. But that is a formality, since all real power is now in the hands of the Israelis and their local allies.

The first step towards pushing Lebanese authority aside was to remove or at least cow the Lebanese security forces. So the Lebanese army has been turned out of its barracks, sometimes forcibly, and its place has been taken by the deserters from that army serving under Saad Haddad. Soldiers and policemen have been disarmed and some have been locked up.

Lebanese Prime Minister Shafik Wazzan had every reason to complain, on 25 July, that Israel was 'crippling the functioning of Lebanese government departments and substituting them with local administrations'. Within the first week of the invasion, Israeli military governors had been appointed for all the towns, and on 14 June Edward Cody reported in the *Guardian* that Israel was moving in 'experienced military and civilian administrators from the West Bank and Gaza Strip to run civilian affairs in the south for a long period'.

Haddad and Other Local Allies

The task of ruling southern Lebanon has been considerably simplified by the eager assistance given to Israel by its local allies — Haddad's 'Free Lebanon Forces' in the area from the frontier northward, and further north the Maronite Phalange. On 10 June Haddad announced (*Jerusalem Post*, 11 June) that he intended 'to incorporate all of the areas taken by the IDF into his "Free Lebanon" '.

Five weeks later it was apparent that he had been as good as his word, or even better. Bernstein and Morris reported (*Jerusalem Post*, 16 July) that Haddad's force had taken over the whole of southern Lebanon from the mouth of the Awali river to Lake Karoun in the Bekaa: 3,000 square kilometres in all. They reported him as saying, from his new headquarters in Sidon city hall, that he would merge his area with the rest of Lebanon only after the PLO and the Syrians were out of Lebanon and a Lebanese-Israeli peace treaty was concluded. His new army of 'something less than 50,000 men' would be financed by a regional revenue system based on port taxes from Tyre and Sidon, a tax on the Zahrani oil refinery and a commercial tax; the Lebanese government would also make a partial contribution.

Israel, he claimed, was '99 per cent' behind him. The reporters concluded that Israel was giving at least tacit support to his new ambitions. This was a loyal, tactful understatement, for Haddad was a creation of the Israelis and wholly dependent on them. But for that, his ambitions would sound absurd. Not only did Israel hand over south Lebanon to his control, but his troops, armed and paid by Israel, were allowed to move north to Beirut, where they took part in the fighting alongside the Israelis, which the Phalange did not.

It was in the area between this newly expanded 'Haddadland' and Beirut

Haddad and Sharon in Sidon (AP)

that the Israelis permitted the Phalange militia to move in behind them, setting up party offices, manning roadblocks and generally running affairs where formerly they had had no presence whatsoever. Haddad was nothing without his armed men, but the Phalange was a well-organised party with a programme and an ideology. As such, it was hated by non-Maronites, not just the Muslims but other Christians too, especially the Greek Orthodox.

By letting loose this controversial force, the Israelis were immediately embroiled in Lebanon's ancient confessional feuds. The Maronite Phalangists started harassing their old enemies, the Druze, in the Shouf area. The Druze appealed to their co-religionists in Israel (many of whom are loyal Israelis) and they in turn, appealed to Begin, who had to order the Israeli army to protect the Lebanese Druze from Israel's Phalangist allies. This was a mere foretaste of what was to come.

Not content with having these two militias — the Phalangists and Haddad's

113

forces – to do their local policing, Israel started to build up two other groups in the south. The first already existed: the Shi'ite militia Al-Amal, which, though it had fought hard against the Israeli army at Nabatieh and Khaldeh, swung over to Israel as a preferable substitute for the PLO in the Shi'ite areas. The other was a new grouping called Al-Ansar, recruited from villagers and armed and uniformed by Israel to perform purely local policing duties, a replacement perhaps for the armed rural Lebanese gendarmerie force.

Thus instead of helping to create a strong, united central Lebanese government, which was one of its declared war aims, Israel was helping to achieve the exact opposite. It was sponsoring and supporting several local centres of power, each of them weak, which it would then play off, one against the other: the classic divide-and-rule policy of any occupying power.

There were already signs of wariness and suspicion between the two Christian groups, the Phalangists and the Haddad militia. During the war Israel had been obliged to arrange a meeting between the Phalange commander Bechir Gemayel and Haddad to work out their respective spheres of influence in the south, an agreement that was breached when Haddad units were brought up to the Beirut front, right next to the Phalangist headquarters.

There were built-in contradictions between the policies of Israel and the Phalangists. The latter were sincere in adhering to their brand of Lebanese Maronite nationalism; hence they never gave their approval to Haddad's 'Free Lebanon', based on deserters from the Lebanese army who had violated their oath of loyalty. Anyone who wanted to be president of all Lebanon would have to suppress Haddad's ambitious separatist ideas, which were fully supported by Israel.

Economic Penetration

On 29 August, Israel state radio reported that farmers in southern Lebanon were complaining that they could not sell their produce in local markets, because they were being undercut by cheaper agricultural produce from Israel dumped in the area. They said they would take their complaint to President Sarkis and President-èlect Gemayel. This was the first indication of the contradictions between the economic policies of Lebanon and Israel.

Within days of the invasion, Israel began working towards the integration of the newly-occupied areas into the economy of Israel, something that it had already succeeded in doing with Haddadland. Branches of Israeli banks were opened in Lebanese towns (with mobile branches for Israeli troops) and the shekel quickly became more or less generally accepted as legal tender.

Offices of the Israeli airline El-Al also started doing business. In early August the first group of Lebanese travel agents visited Israel, as official guests, to encourage package tours to Israeli tourist sites and to arrange for Lebanese citizens in America to spend time in Israel. Coachloads of Israeli tourists started touring southern Lebanon, with armed guards provided by the army.

More important was the fast build-up of commerce between Israel and the occupied southern area. The special 'director of commerce with Lebanon', in the Israeli Ministry of Industry and Trade, was able to announce that in July, while the battle of Beirut still raged, trade with Lebanon exceeded $4 million – or four times the amount of Israel's annual imports from Egypt, excluding oil.

The director predicted that this monthly figure could be doubled in the first year, followed by a period of further steady growth. In fact the figure rose to $8 million in August. But the trade is all one way: Israel, so far, has not imported any goods from Lebanon but has exported food, textiles, plastics and building materials.

All this activity made sense only in the disturbed conditions following the war; once the new President, Amin Gemayel, had settled in, it was expected that his government, as a member of the Arab League, would have to put a stop to this trade and reactivate Lebanon's boycott of Israel, as part of the Arab League boycott. What would happen then, if Haddad, the local overlord, refused to close the southern border? Egypt, of course, had defied the Arab boycott, but Egypt is the largest Arab country and enjoys significant revenues from its oil, from the Suez Canal and from its many workers in Arab lands, whom those countries cannot do without. Lebanon is a small country, dependent on Arab markets and Arab clients for its banking business, its export-import trade and its tourism; and the Lebanese working in Arab countries are not indispensable. Lebanon also needs large funds to rebuild its shattered economy and these can only come from the oil-rich Arab states. They are not going to give large gifts to a Lebanon that defies the general Arab stand towards Israel.

Israel's political ingestion of Lebanon seemed to be complete when Bechir Gemayel was elected president on 23 August. The candidacy of such an openly pro-Israeli leader was possibly only with Israel exerting a major influence on Lebanon's internal affairs. Without the Israeli military presence, the Phalangist militia would not have dared to frog-march into parliament the four reluctant Christian deputies whose presence provided the necessary quorum; and, symbolically, Israeli army officers were present at the military academy where the election was held.

But Bechir Gemayel did not survive; his Israeli connection was his undoing, either because it had been too close or because it was unravelling. Even that stalwart friend of Israel Henry Kissinger said, on 5 October, that Israel had damaged Bechir Gemayel by asking him too insistently and too publicly to sign a peace treaty.

After the Sabra-Chatila massacre it was noticeable that the Israeli media and official spokesmen said, repeatedly, that the Phalangist forces alone had perpetrated the crime and that the Haddad militia had nothing to do with it. Even if this were true it seemed, at the very least, disloyal that Israel should so incriminate the very group with which it had collaborated in allowing the atrocity to happen. The Israeli stance was so odd that several Beirut newspapers speculated that, by accusing the Phalange, Israel was trying to destroy the

Israeli and Lebanese Christian forces together in the south (AP)

chances of Amin Gemayel, the new Phalange leader, being elected president by making it difficult for the Muslims to vote for him. The Muslims ignored the Israeli ploy and voted for Amin, and at the election the Israeli military presence was, this time, conspicuous by its absence.

The Israelis never concealed the fact that they did not much like Amin Gemayel, who was nowhere near as anti-Arab and anti-Palestinian as his brother. So, accepting that they no longer had their man in the presidential palace, the Israelis promptly fell back on the dependent and dependable Haddad, and Sharon made several statements that Israel would continue to back him. The northern frontier of his domain was fixed: his writ would run throughout the territory to the south of the Awali river. Roadblocks at the frontier and throughout this area were manned only by his men.

It is through Haddad that Israel has ingested southern Lebanon, politically and administratively. Thus the Haddad forces do not allow the Lebanese army to move south of the Awali (*L'Orient*, 2 October) nor are any members of the Phalange militia allowed into the area. The police and the civil administration are helped (that is, supervised) by Haddad's men, and Haddad himself said openly (*IHT*, 15 September) that he would retain control of the south until the Beirut government signed a peace treaty with Israel.

Haddad knows his place and keeps to it. In an interview with Robert Fisk

(*The Times*, 23 September), he said that his forces 'do nothing without the co-ordination of the Israeli army'. He repeated this several times. 'To make any individual action is not feasible.' He, too, has been thoroughly ingested by his Israeli patron.

7. The Reason Why

The long-term objective of Israel's onslaught on the Palestinians in Lebanon is to be found in a document submitted by the World Zionist Organisation to the Versailles Conference, in 1919, on the future boundaries of the Jewish homeland. In the carve-up of the Middle East between the victorious Allied Powers after World War I, they found that they had to take into account the dimensions of this amorphous entity that had been promised to the Zionists by the British government in the Balfour Declaration of 1917.

From the start the Zionists, in private, conceived of their 'homeland' as a state with that essential attribute of statehood, international boundaries. After prolonged discussion (described in fascinating detail by the Israeli scholar H.F. Frischwasser-Raanan in his book *The Frontiers of a Nation*) the Zionists proposed that the Jewish state should extend to the following limits.

In the north, the line began at a point just south of Sidon, on the Mediterranean coast, then ran slightly south of the horizontal, right across the Lebanon range and the southern Bekaa Valley to the south-western slope of Mount Hermon, and then to a point not far from Kuneitra, about '20 kilometres south of Damascus'. There it turned due south and continued at a distance of about 10 kilometres west of, and parallel to, the Damascus-Medina railway, up to Maan in southern Jordan, and from there in a straight line to the head of the Gulf of Aqaba.

The state's southern border was not laid down and was to be determined in negotiation with the Egyptians. Why? Because the Zionists hoped that the whole of Sinai might be included in Eretz Israel, the biblical land of Israel.

This delimitation, that has never been renounced by the Zionists, thus comprises almost all of southern Lebanon, including the Litani River, the (Syrian) Golan Heights, and both the east and west banks of the River Jordan.

It is significant that when the State of Israel was proclaimed in 1948, David Ben-Gurion, the first Prime Minister, resisted attempts to define its frontiers, saying that they would run wherever the state was able to establish them. This unique idea of flexible frontiers was captured in a graceful simile produced by the British Zionist, Norman Bentwich, who was to become the first Attorney-General of the British Mandatory Administration in Palestine: the area of the Jewish State, he said, resembled the skin of a deer; when the deer waxes fat the skin expands, when it is lean there is contraction.

The skin of the Jewish State has both expanded and contracted. It expanded in 1948, when the Zionist forces overran areas beyond those given to them under the UN partition plan. The skin expanded again in 1956, when the Israelis captured most of Sinai, only to contract rapidly when they were ordered out by President Eisenhower. It expanded mightily when the Israelis in the 1967 war took Sinai again and the West Bank and the Golan Heights. There was a further expansion on the Golan after the 1973 war, but a contraction, by stages, in the Sinai. The skin expanded once more when, after the 1978 Litani Operation, an Israeli puppet regime was established in a strip along the Lebanese frontier under the nominal control of 'Major' Saad Haddad.

Then, in 1982, there was a large, rapid expansion of territory under Israeli occupation (that is, under the control of Haddad) to a line in the coastal area beyond that laid down in the 1919 plan, but up to the 1919 line in the Bekaa. Elsewhere the 1919 frontier was reached in the Golan, formally annexed to Israel; it will move eastwards to the Jordan River if and when the West Bank is formally annexed, which is the announced intention of the present Israeli government under Menachem Begin, who is firmly of the belief that the area is an integral part of Greater Eretz Israel.

That southern Lebanon should, in some form or other, come under Israeli control or influence is a belief that has been held by many Israeli leaders over the years. In 1948 Ben-Gurion wrote that, after the existing multi-religious Lebanese state was overthrown, 'a Christian state ought to be set up there with its southern frontier on the Litani', thus moving the Israeli frontier north by 20 kilometres.

In 1955 the then Israeli Foreign Minister, Moshe Sharett, recorded this amazingly prophetic scheme of Moshe Dayan:

> According to Dayan the only thing that's necessary is to find a Lebanese officer, even a major will do. We should either win his heart or buy him with money to declare himself the saviour of the Maronite population. Then the Israeli army will enter Lebanon, occupy the necessary territory and create a Christian regime that will ally itself with Israel. The territory from the Litani southwards will be totally annexed to Israel. Dayan recommends that this be done immediately, tomorrow.

In the event, Israel had to wait 23 years before, in 1978, it produced the renegade 'Major' Haddad.

That the Begin regime was not averse to Israeli domination of southern Lebanon was indicated by statements such as one made on 22 December 1981, by Begin's Defence Minister and close collaborator, General Ariel Sharon:

> We have to establish a buffer zone in Lebanon as it is clear that the Lebanese government would do nothing to stop terrorism. The

establishment of such a zone will obviously mean the annexation of part of Lebanese territory.

An even clearer indication of Begin's larger aims came during the war, on 22 July 1982, when the three-member Tehiya Party joined Begin's government. The leading member of this party is the former terrorist Geula Cohen, who obliged the government to declare Jerusalem as Israel's eternal and undivided capital and formally to annex the Golan Heights. For Tehiya, Greater Eretz Israel includes southern Lebanon: its second member, Hanan Porath, claims that the area is actually part of 'the national Patrimony', the 1919 frontier, while Professor Yuval Ne'eman, the third member, would place Israel's 'security border' on the Zahrani River or at least the Litani.

Professor Ne'eman is now a member of the Begin Cabinet and on 24 June 1982, a fortnight after the war began, he laid out his views on southern Lebanon in a long article in the *Jerusalem Post*. He referred to an earlier proposal (allegedly made in 1948 by leaders of the Shia community) for 'the establishment of an autonomous Shia principality in north-western Galilee, on both sides of the Litani River, federated with Israel. Israel must weigh the extent to which the entire Shiite alliance should now be incorporated into the current autonomous area under Major Haddad, or whether it should comprise a separate political unit.'

He concluded,

> A long stay in Lebanon [by the Israeli army] will achieve peace in Galilee. The IDF [Israeli Defence Forces] will also maintain security more faithfully than a multinational force. In the interim, Israel will have an opportunity of reaching a stage of socio-economic development in the nearby region which, geographically and historically, is an integral part of Eretz Israel. Israel could possibly even reach an agreement on border rectification.

It was a month after Ne'eman expressed such expansionist views that Begin took him into his Cabinet.

Obviously all these rearrangements and rectifications in southern Lebanon could only come to pass with the compliance of the Lebanese central government in Beirut. Looking well ahead, Begin began in 1975, the first year of the Lebanese civil war, to develop relations with what has become the Israeli surrogate in Beirut — the Maronite Phalange Party. At first secretly, and then with increasing openness, Israel supplied the Phalangist militia with arms and equipment — tanks, artillery, vehicles, ammunition, uniforms, plus technical advice — which, according to Begin, could by 1982 be valued at $100 million (some sources put the figure at $250 million).

This was a shrewd investment because, according to a politico-religious division established by the French in 1934, based on a fudged 1932 census, the Lebanese president always has to come from the Maronite community, which was alleged at the time to be the largest grouping. Although the

Maronites are now only the third largest community after the Shias and the Sunnis, all effective power remains in the hands of the Maronite President.

Therefore it came as no surprise when Israel let it be known, well before the invasion, that its candidate for president was Bechir Gemayel, the young and ruthless leader of the Phalangist militia, who had made several secret visits to Israel. The *Jerusalem Post* reported, on 9 July 1982, that Sharon did not wish to pull Israeli forces back from Beirut 'until . . . Gemayel is firmly ensconced in the presidential palace'. Likewise, after the invasion, Israel gave Haddad and the Phalangists a free hand to extend their activities and influence in areas occupied by Israeli forces, a process of indirect annexation that is dealt with in greater detail elsewhere in this book.

But this degree of Israeli interference in Lebanon's internal affairs — described by the United States and Israel as 'the re-establishment of a strong and independent Lebanese government' — could only be part of a still wider rearrangement. What that was likely to be was described by Jonathan Frankel, an associate professor in the Hebrew University, in the *Jerusalem Post* (27 June 1982):

> Ariel Sharon, after all, has never sought to keep secret his grand strategy, his three-pronged programme. Lebanon should be cleared of foreign forces [the PLO and the Syrians] and re-established as a Christian-dominated state. The PLO should be effectively destroyed; the occupied territories [West Bank and Gaza] annexed to Israel; the Arab population there granted a highly limited form of internal autonomy; and Jewish settlements vastly expanded. Finally, the Palestinians should be encouraged to overthrow the Hashemite Kingdom and convert Jordan into their own national state.

The Paris daily *Le Matin* reported (2 July) that, three days earlier, Sharon had declared that 'as prime minister he would give King Hussein 24 hours to leave Amman'.

But even this amount of rearrangement by the Israelis of the neighbouring political scene could only endure if it were part of a total and radical regional rearrangement, with the frontiers established after World War I being erased and redrawn. The Israeli plan for a fragmented Middle East, a medley of mini-states, dominated by Israel, actually exists. An important document was published, in Hebrew, in *Kivunim* (Directions) in February 1982, by the World Zionist Organisation, the embodiment of Zionist thinking in Israel and abroad.

The author, Oded Yinon, a former senior officer of the Israeli Foreign Ministry, begins by arguing that all the states of the Middle East are fragile because within their artificial frontiers are grouped antagonistic racial and religious communities who really do not want to live together. This presents Israel with 'far-reaching opportunities for the first time since 1967 . . . today we suddenly face immense opportunities for thoroughly transforming the situation and this we must do in the coming decade, otherwise we shall not survive as a state.'

Sinai must be regained because of its oil and mineral wealth, and this will be possible because 'Egypt is already a corpse, all the more so if we take into account the growing Muslim-Christian rift.' So 'breaking Egypt down territorially into distinct geographical regions is the political aim of Israel in the 1980s on its western front'. These 'regions' would be 'a Christian Coptic state in Upper Egypt alongside a number of weak states' for the Egyptian Muslims.

As regards Jordan:

> Israel's policy, both in peace and in war, ought to be directed at the liquidation of Jordan under the present regime and the transfer of power to the Palestinian majority.

That majority should be increased by 'accelerating the emigration of Palestinians from the West to the East Bank'.

'Lebanon's total dissolution into five provinces that already almost exist serves as a precedent': these 'provinces' would comprise a Christian Maronite-dominated area, a Muslim area, a Druze area, a fourth dominated by Syria and a fifth, mainly Shia, under Israeli control through Haddad's militia.

'The dissolution of Syria and Iraq later on into ethnically or religiously unique areas such as in Lebanon, is Israel's primary target on the eastern front.' Syria will be divided into a coastal 'Shiite Alawite state, a Sunni state in the Aleppo area, another Sunni state in Damascus hostile to its northern neighbour, and the Druze will set up a state maybe even in our Golan, and certainly in the Hauran and northern Jordan. This state will be the guarantee of peace and security in the area in the long run, and that aim is already within our reach today.'

Iraq is 'a definite candidate as one of Israel's targets', with 'the higher aim of breaking Iraq up into its denominations, a provincial division on ethnic religious grounds' into 'three or more states around Basra, Baghdad and Mosul, and the Shiite areas in the south will separate from the Sunni and Kurdish north'. 'The entire Arabian peninsula is a natural candidate for dissolution', though Yinon does not provide a detailed forecast.

This Zionist blueprint for Israeli expansion is, of course, based on a revival of the millet, or communal, system of the Ottoman Empire, on which nostalgic glances have been cast by such pro-Israeli and right-wing academics as Bernard Lewis and Elie Kedourie. The anti-Zionist intellectual Noam Chomsky took the World Zionist Organisation plan sufficiently seriously to refer to it in an article in *The Guardian* (7 July 1982) and, projecting further into the future, suggested that 'the long-term objective may be an alliance of Iran (now restored to the West), Turkey and Israel, ruling the region in alliance with the United States — the ultimate source of their power.'

On 21 June Begin proclaimed that the Israeli attack on Lebanon, launched a few weeks earlier, was 'not an invasion', because Israel did not intend to occupy or annex Lebanon (even though this had been going on for four years in Haddadland). To this cynical claim by Begin an equally cynical reply was made by a columnist in the right-wing Israeli newspaper *Yediot Ahronot* (9 July): 'Entering in order to get out is not an invasion, just as forced entry and withdrawal is not rape.'

It is to the credit of the Israeli public, or rather that 30% of it that is said to oppose the war, that it recognised very early on, in the war's third or fourth day, that this war was different in character from Israel's four earlier wars in 1948, 1956, 1967 and 1973. Those, the theory goes, were defensive wars, while this was a war deliberately contrived and initiated for reasons that had little or nothing to do with the defence of Israel.

This view was expressed most succinctly by the Israeli novelist Amos Oz (*Davar*, 22 June):

> For the first time . . . we have gone to war not in order to fight for our existence, but in order to get rid of a nuisance and in order to change this whole region.

A letter addressed to Begin declared:

> It is clear to me that I have been deceived and that I have been called to the first war in Israel's history which was not a war of defence but a dangerous gamble to achieve political goals.

It was signed by 35 soldiers of the elite commando unit that had carried out the Entebbe raid of which Israel is so proud.

That all four of Israel's earlier wars were defensive is, however, a myth; those of 1956 and of 1967 were equally contrived acts of aggression; but even Israeli critics do not go further than comparing the present war with the 1956 attack on Suez. Israel's leaders have not hidden the fact that they had been preparing the attack on Lebanon for a long time.

Defence Minister Sharon has said (*Jerusalem Post*, 9 July) that he had been 'planning this operation since I took office' (in July 1981). On 12 August Sharon told the Knesset that he had secretly visited Beirut in January 1982 to make his plans on the spot. Chief-of-Staff General Eitan told the Israeli press 'that operational planning for "Peace for Galilee" started eight months ago.'

Defenders of the war have not even tried to hide or excuse the fact that it is a non-defensive war. Thus Gideon Hausner, a former Attorney-General and Cabinet Minister, in an article entitled, without cynicism, 'Victory for Humanity' (the *Jerusalem Post*, 11 July), says with relief,

> For the first time since the founding of the Jewish state we were able to plan a campaign not as a result of foreign aggression, as in 1948, 1967, 1973, and it was one free from the restraints of embarrassing partners as in 1956. Israel has proved again its dedication, its power and its respect for human values.

Hausner was the prosecutor of Adolf Eichmann.

Begin himself, speaking to a group of disabled veterans on 18 July drew a distinction between this war and the defensive wars Israel had been compelled to fight.

> The Prime Minister stressed that wars Israel has had to fight from a lack of alternative were more costly in casualties, citing the War of Independence [1948] and the Yom Kippur War [1973]. We must learn that we shall not always fight for lack of an alternative, Begin said, and we must know how to weigh our security and occasionally go to war.

In the testimony of the Israeli soldiers protesting against the war one phrase keeps recurring. Thus in *Davar* (28 June):

> Our feeling was that they broke the rules of the game according to which the Israeli army used to operate as an army that is supposed to defend our existence, and they are going to turn it into a political policeman.

Again in *Al-Hamishmar* (2 July):

> All the rules of the game have been broken in this war. They took the Israeli Defence Forces and turned it into an occupation army for political aims.

The Israeli leadership, however, sought to give the war religious sanctifica-tion. On 8 June the Chief Rabbinate, headed by the Ashkenazi and Sephardic chief rabbis, an integral part of the Israeli establishment, decreed that the invasion was 'a divinely inspired war', *milhemet mitzva*, meriting 'divine sanction'.

In short, this was a holy war, the Jewish equivalent of the Islamic *jihad*, something the Israelis scorn and condemn when proclaimed by their Muslim enemies. In that same proclamation the rabbis also recommended a daily public reading of Psalm 83, a psalm full of dire curses on the enemies of the Chosen People. In late June the Rabbinate also ruled that the operation in all of its stages and operations was a 'moral war of a high order' and was distinguished by the restraint with which soldiers used their arms in order to avoid harming innocent victims.

On 28 July, during the siege of Beirut, Chief Rabbi Goren reiterated that the war was not only a just war but an obligatory one; that according to *Halacha*, Jewish religious law, the Israeli army was permitted to enter the city because, according to Talmudic injunction, he who begins a *mitzva* must finish it, in this case by destroying the PLO's headquarters in Beirut.

Goren concluded that a war of obligation must be fought against any enemy who threatens a border settlement in Eretz Israèl, or threatens a Jewish community anywhere in the world. Ten days earlier Begin's office had described the war as being 'divinely ordained'.

Two incidents reveal what this concept of a Jewish *jihad* means and what it can lead to. The Rabbinate is represented in the Israeli armed forces by the Military Rabbinate Brigade. In July this unit issued a leaflet to the troops in Lebanon (*Ha'aretz*, 8 August) containing a strange map showing all of Lebanon and a good part of western Syria. No borders are shown, either between Israel and Lebanon and Syria, or between Lebanon and Syria; all the towns and villages are designated only by ancient Biblical names: thus Beirut becomes Be'erot (Hebrew for 'wells').

The caption below reads: 'The one who looks at this map will see that the shore cities of Lebanon, the central plateau and a significant part of the Bekaa are the possession of the Tribe of Asher.' This is followed by a quotation from the Book of Joshua, Chapter 19: 'From the mountains of Shouf till Sidon the inheritance of the families of the Tribe of Asher.'

The implication is clear: if this area belonged and still belongs to Asher, one of the Twelve Tribes of Israel, it belongs to the State of Israel today. *Ha'aretz* accordingly headed the item: 'This Is Ours – And That Too'. The author, Yitzhak Shteiner, military rabbi, goes on at some length to draw comparisons with a campaign waged by Joshua (described in Joshua, Chapter 11), when 3,200 years ago he made a 'preventive' attack northwards on three axes, western, central and eastern, just as the Israeli army did in June 1982.

In the Jerusalem daily *Kol Ha'ir* (reported by *Ha'aretz*, 24 June), the Chief Sephardic Rabbi of Jerusalem, Shalom Mashash, considered whether it was permissible to give non-Jewish blood to wounded Israeli soldiers. It was permissible, he said, to do so only when the injured person's life was in danger: 'However it is obvious that one must refuse non-Jewish blood from the beginning; it takes Jewish blood to cure Jews.'

Not only was this Israel's first non-defensive war it was also the first that had been unpopular inside Israel. There was not the usual supportive consensus in Israeli public opinion, or in the Knesset, or even within the cabinet. This had been essentially a war contrived and implemented by two men – Begin and Sharon.

To them was applied, for the first time, that singularly damning epithet 'Judeo-Nazi' – and by other Israelis. Thus an Israeli soldier from a tank unit: 'I think that Sharon is putting us into the family of nations that includes the Nazis' (*Al-Hamishmar*, 2 July). Or this much earlier testimony on Begin from Ben-Gurion, Israel's first and greatest Prime Minister, in a letter in May 1963: 'Begin is a thoroughly Hitlerite type, ready to destroy all the Arabs . . . I have no doubt that Begin hates Hitler but this hatred does not prove that he is different from him . . . when for the first time I heard Begin on the radio, I heard the voice and the screeching of Hitler.'

How can someone so passionately concerned for the safety of the Israelis, and of Jews elsewhere, be so contemptuous of, and indifferent to, the sufferings of non-Jewish people? In the Knesset on 8 June Begin, referring to the Palestinians, said, 'We shall defend our children. If the hand of a two-legged animal is raised against them, it will be severed.'

One explanation of Begin's philosophy is that it is the result of his mystical beliefs, derived from the school of the *kabbala*. According to these beliefs, as interpreted by Begin, the Jewish God, Jewish law, and the Jewish people form a trinity: an attack on the people is therefore an attack on God, for which no punishment can be too severe. But Jewish attacks on non-Jews are simply acts of God, something that happens, sometimes necessarily so.

Sharon is an altogether simpler character: he is merely an insatiably ambitious, power-hungry politician who uses the army as a springboard. To him Ben-Gurion once put the question: 'Well, Arik, have you stopped telling lies?' (Reported by David Landau, the *Jerusalem Post*, 25 June.)

One of his peers, General Haim Herzog, writes of him in his recent book *The Arab-Israeli Wars*: 'He was to be accused of insubordination and dishonesty . . . few, if any, of his superior officers over the years had a good word to say of him as far as human relations and integrity were concerned.'

So, too, some of his junior officers. Hirsh Goodman (*Jerusalem Post*, 26 June) recounts how, during the Sinai campaign in 1956, four young battalion commanders including Gur, later a chief-of-staff, and Eitan, the present incumbent, accused their commanding officer, Sharon, of senselessly sending young men to their deaths and of exceeding his orders.

In addition to the larger motivations for the attack on Lebanon there were other more immediate reasons – above all the need to distract Israeli public opinion from external and domestic failures by the classic device of launching a foreign adventure. The calculation was that the large-scale employment of the Israeli Defence Forces, Zahal, was bound to bring about a closing of ranks behind the Begin government. Zahal was the only universally respected institution in the state; the adventure would be immune from criticism because to criticise it would be to criticise Zahal, which would be unacceptable, even treasonable. The same argument was later used against Israeli critics of the war.

The 'Peace for Galilee' operation was supposed to have been caused by the PLO's breach of the ceasefire negotiated by US mediator Philip Habib in July 1981. In fact, the first of the proximate causes of the operation was the exact opposite – it was launched because the ceasefire had been holding.

An Israeli scholar, Professor Yehoshua Porath, has explained this point with percipience (*Ha'aretz*, 25 June):

> I think the Israeli government's decision (or to be more exact, its two leaders' decision) resulted from the fact that the ceasefire had held . . . Yasser Arafat had succeeded in doing the impossible. He managed an indirect agreement, through American mediation, with Israel and even managed to keep it for a whole year . . . this was a disaster for Israel.
> If the PLO agreed upon and maintained a ceasefire they may in the future agree to a more far-reaching political settlement and maintain that too.
> If in the future we shall be closer to negotiations with other Arab bodies, apart from Egypt, will the Israeli government be able to claim

that the PLO is no more than a wild gang of murderers, who are not legitimate negotiating partners? Won't there be pressure to include the PLO in future negotiations over the future of the territories occupied in 1967?

Writing in the third week of the war, but looking ahead, Professor Porath said:

Our government hopes that after losing their logistic territorial base the PLO shall go back to terror methods, lay bombs all over the world, hijack planes and murder many Israelis. Thus it would lose much of the political legitimacy it had gained, the Israelis would be unified in hate and disgust towards it, and the possibility of the development of a moderate body on the Palestinian side that could be a legitimate negotiating partner would be prevented.

The prospect that the PLO should achieve respectability and legitimacy alarms Israel. The very word 'Palestine' tolls for them like a funeral knell, because evidently the Palestinians and the Israelis cannot both be legitimate possessors of the Land of Israel. Hence the Israelis insist that the PLO should not merely accept Israel's existence but its *right* to exist, a novelty in diplomatic procedure.

A second reason was the fact that immigration to Israel was falling and emigration rising. There was the well-publicised fact that 90% of the Jews leaving Russia chose not to go to Israel, despite Israeli attempts to force them to do so. Official statistics show that in the first six months of 1982 there was a net outflow of almost 20,000 Jews from Israel, nearly the same as the 1981 figure for the same period. The official immigration figure for 1981, a total of 13,000 people, was the lowest for 29 years. Israel is an ideological state: by packing their bags and leaving it Jews were depriving it of its ideological raison d'etre.

A third, psychological, reason for the attack was given by Begin when he said that Operation Peace for Galilee was needed 'to heal the trauma of the Yom Kippur War'. Israel was severely jolted in the first days of that war, in October 1973, when it seemed that the Arab armies, especially the Syrians, were going to break through into Israel itself. By taking the initiative to attack, Israel's image would be restored. There was also the need to make up for what was called the 'loss' of Sinai, handed back to Egypt in April 1982. If Israel had to withdraw from the south, it would advance in the north.

A fourth, political, reason was the failure of the Camp David process. It had been clear almost from the outset that no other Arab state was going to join the process and make peace with Israel; likewise the discussions with the Egyptians on Palestinian autonomy had been stalemated for two years: so Israel was under no restraint to act moderately towards its hostile Arab neighbours. The blocking of the peace option made the war option that much more tempting.

A fifth reason was that the administration in Washington was the most friendly Israel had ever had. Secretary of State Haig seemed prepared to back the Israelis all the way. Moreover, the Arabs had never been more weak and divided. Egypt's separate peace with Israel had taken the largest and strongest Arab state out of the fighting line. Differences over Saudi Arabia's Fahd Plan, a reasonable alternative to Camp David, had brought about the total collapse of the Arab summit in Fez in November 1981. The Iran-Iraq war had widened the splits in the Arab camp, with some Arab states, notably Syria, actively supporting non-Arab Iran against Arab Iraq. Consequently there was no danger that the Arabs could unite and resist an Israeli attack on the PLO in Lebanon.

The sixth and final reason was Israel's parlous economic situation, similar to the depression that immediately preceded, and precipitated, the 1967 war. The laissez-faire economic policies of the right-wing Begin government had not provided any answer to Israel's deep-seated ills. The annual inflation rate was 130% and the balance-of-payments deficit about $4,000 million. The treasury had been printing almost three billion Israel Shekels ($120 million) a month to bridge the gap between its revenue and its expenditure. Jewish investment from abroad had declined to a trickle. The 1967 war turned Israel's economy round from depression to boom: why shouldn't the war of 1982 do the same?

We have dealt with the reasons for the Israeli attack and with its immediate causes. The actual pretext, however, was the PLO's breach of Habib's 1981 ceasefire when it shelled and rocketed northern Israel on 4 and 5 June. In the course of this bombardment there was just one death, and that was of an old man — from heart-failure.

The bombardment was the PLO's response to a massive Israeli air attack on Beirut on 4 and 5 June, in which over 200 were killed, following the shooting of Israeli Ambassador Argov in London on 3 June. Israel immediately accused the PLO of being guilty of the shooting. According to the London police, however, the shooting was the work of an anti-PLO group, led by Abu Nidal, which has made more than one attempt to kill Arafat; the PLO representative in London was on the gunmen's death list.

However flimsy the pretext, it worked because the Israeli bombing succeeded in pushing the PLO into retaliation. Two previous Israeli attempts in April and May, and several earlier ones, had failed. On 21 April the Israeli airforce had attacked targets in southern Lebanon, killing 35, in reaction to the death of an Israeli soldier when his vehicle hit a mine inside Lebanon (where Israeli soldiers were not supposed to be). The PLO took no retaliatory military action. On 9 May the Israelis bombed again, killing six, because of four incidents in Lebanon and Israel in which a soldier and a woman and two children were slightly wounded. This time the PLO fired back into northern Israel, but because they deliberately avoided aiming at settlements, as the Israeli press noted, there were no Israeli casualties.

The restraint shown by the PLO in these two earlier incidents, a restraint imposed by Arafat, was strongly contested within the PLO, and made full-scale retaliation certain after the third Israeli provocation on 4 and 5 June. However, the PLO shelling on these two days, which Begin and Sharon described as 'intolerable' and 'unbearable', killed not one Israeli.

Israel had never liked the Habib ceasefire. It had blocked the implementation of the attack on Lebanon that Sharon and Eitan had been planning since July 1981. It had put Israel into a negotiating partnership with the PLO. Worse still, the ceasefire had been observed by the PLO, as affirmed by President Reagan on 30 June and by a British Minister of State for Foreign Affairs on 22 June.

Moreover the Americans had not accepted Israel's view that the ceasefire was world-wide: the US, the Lebanese government and the PLO maintained that the agreement applied only to military activity across the Lebanese-Israel border, and not, as Israel claimed, to attacks on Israelis abroad, or civilian targets in Israel and the occupied territories; nor did it expressly forbid a PLO build-up in southern Lebanon.

By giving the ceasefire world-wide application, and by going back several years, Sharon was able to put forward impressive figures for the numbers of Israelis and Jews killed by the PLO. These fictions have been mercilessly analysed and ridiculed in the Israeli press.

Thus *Ha'aretz* on 30 June reported Sharon's claim that, since the 1960s, Israel had suffered 1,002 casualties as a result of 'terrorist' actions. It noted that, in reality, since 1967, in all 106 Israelis had been killed. The annual number was indeed declining — 20 in 1980, 17 in 1981 and one in 1982. During those three years more than 1,200 Israelis had been killed in traffic accidents.

Later, Sharon produced the even larger figure of 1,392 killed since 1967 (*Ha'aretz*, 16 July). A *Ha'aretz* reporter, B. Michael, reported that a retired Israeli police officer, after going through the archives, proved that the number of civilians killed in that period was 282. To these Sharon had added the 285 Israeli soldiers killed in action against the PLO, the great majority outside Israel's borders; 392 Arabs from the West Bank and Gaza killed in security incidents, some blown up by their own explosives; and 326 citizens of other countries killed by some terrorist organisation or other, allegedly affiliated to the PLO.

'I would not be astonished', said the reporter, 'to find Moro and Lord Mountbatten numbered among them.' (Even these figures do not add up to 1,392).

In his press conference on 30 June President Reagan, referring to the events preceding the Israeli attack, said, 'We were caught as much by surprise as anyone, and we wanted a diplomatic solution, and believed there could have been one.' There could never have been one, because Israel's armed forces, under Begin, Sharon and Eitan, had been geared for an attack on Lebanon for many months. Only a pretext was needed. Once one was found, the massive Israeli military machine lunged forward into Lebanon.

8. The Failure of Success

The harmful effects on Israel of the 'Peace for Galilee' operation are so many and varied that a book could be written on that aspect of the war alone. The violence and blood-letting of any war cannot but have a strong effect on the society waging it and that has been true of Israel's wars as well as those of other countries. The 1967 war, by vastly extending Israel's territory, implanted in it the colonial mentality; the 1973 war, which scared the Israelis by revealing their military vulnerability, produced, paradoxically, a hunger for overwhelming military might with a growing obsessive doubt that they could ever achieve security through such might.

But the 1982 campaign has had an incomparably more profound impact than any of the earlier conflicts, because it has called into question the moral basis of the state; not just its character, but its raison d'etre.

Before examining the failures of the campaign it is fair to consider the claims of Israel's war leaders — Begin, Sharon and Eitan, especially the two latter — that the operation was a success. The more general reasons given for why Israel went to war, are mentioned in the last chapter. General Eitan wanted to use his large and expensive war machine, and he has used it; the army wanted a new generation of soldiers with battle experience and it has one; Begin spoke of the need to exorcise the trauma of the 1973 war and compared with what happened in Lebanon that war now looks like a picnic.

But even these 'achievements' were diminished by their side-effects; the way Israel's war machine was used earned it universal reprobation; the new generation of 'blooded' soldiers turned against the blood-letting; and the trauma of 1973 has been replaced with worse nightmares. There is the military accomplishment in that the Israeli army advanced to Beirut and even beyond it: it entered its first Arab capital. But it will have to leave most of that territory, as it has already had to begin withdrawal from Beirut; when it does the IDF will leave behind a populace with no illusions.

The other military achievement of the operation was proof that the weapons used by the Israelis were superior to those provided by Russia to the Syrians. But the Israeli weapons were US-supplied and US experts doubted Israel's claim that Israeli technology improved on the American originals.

What does this leave of the three officially-proclaimed objectives of the campaign? The first, to push PLO fighters out of bombardment range of northern Galilee, has been achieved (though this had already been achieved by diplomatic means through the ceasefire arranged by Habib in July 1981). Nevertheless, security in Galilee is undoubtedly more assured than before.

But the question remains: who is to do the assuring? Because of the way the war has gone the old assumption that the Israeli army would remain in southern Lebanon seems no longer tenable: a prolonged Israeli occupation is no longer acceptable to anyone. Even Sharon said that the IDF will have to hand over to some other force, which will not do the job as efficiently as would the IDF.

The measure of Israel's success in attaining its first public objective will be gauged according to which force is eventually placed in southern Lebanon. If it is the Haddad militia the Israeli success will be considerable; if it is a multi-national force the Israelis can consider they have had only partial success; if it is Unifil Israel must consider it has failed to achieve its first objective, because Unifil's reinstatement would be a continuation of the status quo ante.

Israel's second objective — to smash and uproot the political and military infrastructure of the PLO in Lebanon — has also been achieved, in the sense that the armed forces and political offices of the various groups are no longer in southern Lebanon and Beirut. But the political presence of the PLO continues in Beirut, because the PLO office and the PLO Research Centre, ransacked and looted by the Israelis, have both resumed work.

Paradoxically, the setback in Lebanon has given the PLO greater prestige and influence abroad even before the Sabra-Chatila massacre. This was expressed, in negative terms, by William Pfaff (IHT, 18 September): 'There is no longer a PLO military threat to Israel. There is now a political threat, on a scale which never before existed.'

Israel's third objective, a peace treaty with a strong and stable Lebanon, seemed to have been achieved when Bechir Gemayel was elected president: it became less certain after his 1 September meeting with Begin in northern Israel, and disappeared entirely when Bechir was assassinated and succeeded by his less pro-Israeli brother. Israel acknowledged that fact by repeatedly stating that signing a peace treaty with Lebanon was no longer a precondition for Israel's withdrawal from Lebanon.

Conversely, the adverse effects produced by the war have been immense. The most obvious are economic. On 29 July the Israeli Prime Minister said the war had cost $1.2 billion. Christopher Walker (*The Times,* 30 July) reported that 'some financial experts regard the estimate as conservative, claiming that the true figure — including indirect cost — is nearer to $1,600 million' ($1.6 billion). That estimate came before the prolonged, intense and very expensive bombardment of Beirut.

The Israeli Finance Minister estimated that each 175mm gun shell cost $880 and a tank shell between $272 and $664. Thus the cost of the war from June to October could not be less than $3 billion. Because the US administration became critical of the war, the Israeli government dared not ask for a compensatory increase in its annual aid request, which amounted to \$3 billion. Israel will thus have to foot the war bill itself from an economy with an annual inflation rate of 130% and a balance-of-payments deficit of \$4 billion.

The Israeli government has said it will raise \$1.5 billion in new domestic taxes. But, as Philip Geyelin put it (*Washington Post*, 25 September): 'in doing so, Israel is also raising a question for some congressional critics: if Israel is rich enough to . . . pay for the Lebanon sortie out-of-pocket, what does that say about its need for American aid at current levels?'

Emboldened by the swing in American public opinion against Israel, those 'congressional critics' have, for the first time, talked about cutting back on the huge sums given to Israel every year. A proposal before Congress to convert a \$300-million loan to an outright grant was shelved; as was a separate increase of \$125 million in economic grants. As a result of the war Israel will have to pay more – while receiving less. The Israeli journalist David Krivine (*Jerusalem Post,* 9 July) referred to the 'if inflation doubles' possibility. One major economic war casualty was Israel's national airline, El-Al, shut down in October because of strikes due to post-war hardship.

More damaging than the economic consequences were the political consequences, both abroad and at home. The massacre at Sabra-Chatila became the last straw for world public opinion, which had become increasingly critical of Israel's behaviour during the preceding three and a half months. No government, no organisation of repute came to Israel's defence. Reporting on a visit to Australia, Hirsch Goodman said (*Jerusalem Post, international edition,* 26 September–2 October): 'There were times, many times, when the hostility was almost too much to bear . . . Even genuine friends are questioning whether Israel has not gone completely mad.'

Cartoons and editorials from China to Peru, many in publications hitherto friendly to Israel, presented it no longer as David but as Goliath. Listing some of Israel's political losses the Israeli daily *Al-Hamishmar* (15 July) mentioned, 'we have lost Alexander Haig . . . the American Secretary of State most convenient to Israel; we have lost Mitterrand, the first pro-Israeli French President; we have lost the support of the West European social democrats; we have lost status in the eyes of the policy makers in Washington.'

William Pfaff (*IHT,* 18 September) asserted that, because of the move into West Beirut, 'the Pope, President Reagan, the presidents of Greece, Italy and France and other West Europeans . . . have acknowledged that a Palestinian political entity must be re-created . . . it will inevitably be at the expense of Israel'.

During a visit to Cairo, the British Foreign Secretary called on Israel to change its 'aggressive' attitude towards its Arab neighbours and asserted that the Palestinians should be able to choose between all options, 'including statehood', which, before March, was not a possibility Britain considered.

Events in Lebanon dealt a particularly heavy blow to Israel's relations with Egypt. Though Egypt said it would not denounce the peace treaty with

Israel President Mubarak issued some strong statements of denunciation and said that talks on West Bank autonomy would not be resumed until Israeli troops were withdrawn from Lebanon; the Egyptian ambassador in Tel-Aviv was withdrawn and commercial relations and tourism virtually ceased.

Throughout the war and its aftermath Israel's Prime Minister has tried to convey the impression that he was not worried about world public opinion. But there have been two key developments in the outside world which he could not ignore: the loss of support from the US government and the American Jewish community. Though disapproving, the US administration had expressed a singularly mild reaction to the violations of its arms-supply agreements requiring Israel to use US-supplied armaments for defensive purposes only. After the Sabra-Chatila massacre, emboldened by a clear swing in American public opinion, President Reagan increased efforts to secure internal and international support for his peace plan, rejected by the Begin government, which called for, inter alia, an end to Israel's policy of imposing its sovereignty on the West Bank, and a freeze on Israeli settlements in the occupied territories. Thus the President and the Israeli government reached a state of head-on confrontation.

The Reagan plan also revealed the divisions and disquiet within the American Jewish community. The four leading US Zionist organisations said the plan had its good points and should be discussed, while Israel refused to consider it even as a basis for discussion. After Begin initially refused to set up a commission of enquiry into the massacre at Sabra and Chatila, 150 leading American Jews, including the novelist and Nobel prizewinner Saul Bellow, published a statement highly critical of the Begin government. On this issue the American Jewish community was rent in two, for the first time, and the split has been vehemently public.

This erosion of support has lessened Israel's grip on Washington. Israel could not afford to repeatedly ignore representations from Washington and count on the pro-Israeli American public to be forever tolerant.

On three occasions the US showed it could bend Israel to its will. The first was on 12 August, when the President ordered Begin to stop the bombardment of Beirut – and it was stopped within half an hour (10 minutes, by one account). The second when the Americans insisted that Israeli troops leave West Beirut and Israel tried to lay down conditions which were ignored by a firmly insistent US. When Israel tried to delay its pull-out from Beirut international airport, again trying to impose conditions, it was obliged to leave unconditionally.

Such assertions of American will, the first since 1956, were dangerous for Israel because they meant that their influence on the White House, Congress and State Department had been eroded. Having succeeded on these three occasions, the US administration was more likely to impose its will on the Israeli government in future. Indeed President Reagan stated that he intended to push on with his peace plan despite the negative Israeli government reaction.

The second significant development outside Israel has been increased anti-Jewish feeling in many countries expressed in vandalism and violence against Jewish institutions and offices. Overseas Jewish communities' reaction to events in Lebanon was sufficiently different from those of the population at large to call attention to the normally well-integrated Jewish minorities. There were many individual exceptions, but most Jews chose to follow their traditional pro-Zionist leaders, criticising mildly, remaining silent or even trying to condone Israel's actions when general indignation against such actions was running high.

Any such development inevitably puts Jewish communities at risk. Sensing this, many Jewish community leaders visited Israel during the summer of 1982 and urged Begin and Sharon to remember that what they did and said affected Jews everywhere.

The differences of opinion in the American Jewish community were only a pale reflection of the profound cleavage within Israeli society produced by the massacre. One half of the country was swept by a personal feeling of shame and revulsion while the other appeared not to care.

Time magazine (4 October) called Israel 'A Shaken Nation' and the *Jerusalem Post* (international edition, 26 September–2 October) carried the headline 'Nation in Trauma'. Predictably, political parties took the sides their interests dictated, but not the Israeli people: families and friendships were divided on the issue of whether Israel was in any way responsible for the massacres, whether a public enquiry should be held, whether Israel should get out of Beirut quickly and out of Lebanon altogether.

The press took sides, with Israel's two quality newspapers *Ha'aretz* and *Ma'ariv*, both independent but with very different political attitudes, both critical of the Begin government. Hanna Semer, editor of *Davar*, who was consistently critical of the Lebanon invasion from the beginning, on 20 September, the day after Yom Kippur, the most sacred Day of Atonement, expressed some of the anger and personal anguish that one portion of the population experienced:

> The Prime Minister went to synagogue yesterday. Instead he should have gone to the Presidential Residence, to tender his resignation and thus free Israel and the Jewish people from the curse of this government which has turned our image into that of a monster. The Prime Minister could go to synagogue for Morning Services, Morning Additional Services, Afternoon Services and Evening Services – during every one of the Ten Days of Atonement – and he will still fail to atone for his sin.
>
> This latest horror in Beirut, described by a pro-Israeli American journalist as 'Israel's Babi Yar', followed closely upon the wanton shelling and bombardment of Beirut . . . we shall have to live with these terrible memories . . . I too went to synagogue yesterday. I had the feeling that He to whom we were praying was not among us, that He was in the Shatila refugee camp with the mourners . . . The government must resign, but it will not . . . But we will not remain

silent even if they shower us with tons of tear-gas . . . there will come a day we will all send back our Israeli identity cards, because this is not the way we want to be identified.

Begin was an adroit politician, but he clearly misjudged Israeli reaction to the massacre. The first government reaction, in a Cabinet statement, was to apply the label 'blood libel' to charges that Israel bore responsibility; the second was to refuse a public enquiry because, Begin said, to set one up was to accept a portion of guilt.

The demand for an enquiry became the focus for widespread and ferocious protest. Among those joining in were the President of Israel and his predecessors; the Bar Association; 27 former Israeli ambassadors; 100 poets, writers and literary editors; 200 scientists from the Weizmann Institute; and 350,000 Israelis who attended a rally in Tel-Aviv. This figure represents 10% of the population of Israel, and if everyone who had wanted to attend had been able to do so, the figure would have risen to half a million — one Israeli in six — a referendum against the policies of Begin and Sharon.

Only when Begin agreed to a full public enquiry did the protests subside; but whatever the findings, the damage to Israel's democratic system by Begin's and Sharon's conduct of the war is already visible and will remain. Israeli politics have always been factional but the war has polarised the parties into total antagonism. The idea of a 'loyal opposition' has vanished.

The war has shown that the Cabinet system does not work in Israel, as two men have virtually excluded the rest of the cabinet from the conduct of the war and run it as their own private campaign. More than one Israeli political analyst said that, since June, Israel had become an oligarchy, with the potential danger of becoming a one-man dictatorship under Sharon.

The most serious development for the future of Israeli democracy was that, with the country at war its soldiers came out in public protest against the civilian government. They even formed their own protest groups — 'Soldiers against Silence' and 'There's a Limit'. These groups, demonstrating outside the Defence Ministry, shouted slogans such as 'Purge the army of war criminals', 'Begin's a terrorist'. In two separate meetings, one in Sharon's presence, 100 Israeli top ranking officers called on the Defence Minister to resign. One thousand officers and men signed a public declaration that they did not want to serve in Lebanon. These actions were close to mutiny.

What is left in Israel of that almost mystical respect for civilian authority which deters the men with the guns from imposing their will on their civilian rulers? Until June 1982 that question had never been raised in Israel. It is also in question whether Israeli armed forces can ever again be used in a non-defensive war, or whether that powerful weapon will turn against the politician who uses it for aggressive purposes. At the least the war-minded politician would have to produce a convincing pretext and be more mindful than Begin and Sharon of causing civilian casualties on the other side.

Although this war has put the democratic process at risk in Israel, it has also vindicated itself: it was the people of Israel who pressured the Begin government, and Begin himself, to establish the committee of enquiry. And that pressure was developed and expressed through newspapers which remained free to criticise. The Begin government has indicated such freedom as proof of its devotion to democracy (although strict censorship was observed concerning the conduct of the campaign). But perhaps the tide of public opinion and criticism was running so strongly that the government dared not try to curb it. Whatever the reason, it was to Israel's credit that democratic freedoms were maintained during these turbulent months.

Israel's permanent losses from this war are on the moral plane. Outside Israel the loss is that of credibility. Israel's word is now devalued because its government gave assurances that it failed to keep, and worse, it deceived the United States, its only friend, in such a way that the US was compromised with other governments. As part of the Habib plan, Israel promised the US that it would not advance into West Beirut, would withdraw south of the airport and ensure that the Palestinian camps were protected. The Americans believed these promises and got the Lebanese government and the PLO to accept them: Israel broke them all. Hence the report that when the US mediator returned to Beirut after the massacre he asked the Lebanese Prime Minister, Chafiq Wazzan, 'Do you want to hit me?' Great powers do not like being fooled or, worse, made to look foolish in the eyes of others.

In Israel the moral basis of the state, the contract between the rulers and the ruled, has been undermined: the rulers have been caught lying to the ruled. The Begin government deceived the Israeli people by saying that the purpose of 'Operation Peace for Galilee' was peace in Galilee; and again, following the departure of the PLO fighters, when it said it never intended to enter Beirut, yet was already preparing to do so. It lied in denying knowledge of, and complicity in, the Sabra-Chatila massacre.

When the report of the commission of enquiry is published heads will roll, but even then public trust may have been irreparably damaged. The government lied, within the first 36 hours of the war, on something particularly sacrosanct in Israel, the casualties suffered by the armed forces. Begin and Sharon declared that Beaufort Castle had been taken without casualties, contrary to the facts known to everyone in the forces and to the families of the fallen soldiers. Thereafter the claims of the military spokesmen were suspect in the minds of the men in uniform. Questions have even been raised in Israel about the final death toll of 368 killed: in the first week of July the magazine *Ha'olam Ha'zeh* said that, according to its own research, the figure was just over 1,000.

Judaism in the Jewish State, that is its official institutions, the religious establishment, is a victim of the war, because the Chief Rabbinate declared as a Holy War an invasion that many Israelis believe to be unholy in concept and execution. The two Chief Rabbis were wise enough to make no further declarations on the nature of the war after the massacre.

From its inception many Israelis were worried that Israeli society would be split by what was called 'the Kultur Kampf': the gap between the religious and secular elements, due to the fact that many Jews in the Jewish State were not practising Jews. The internal split produced by this war was infinitely worse — a racial split between the Ashkanazi and the Sephardi sectors of the population.

Eric Silver (*Observer,* 3 October) graphically described the split when he said that the only Sephardis at the mass demonstration in Tel-Aviv protesting the war and the massacre were the ice-cream sellers. The protestors were nearly all white-skinned, educated, middle- and upper-middle class Jews of European descent. Those loyal to Begin and Sharon were brown-skinned, less educated, lower-middle class Jews from the Arab countries. There were exceptions, notably President Navon, a Sephardi who made known his opposition to the war; and at the height of the protest movement some Orthodox Jews demonstrated outside Jerusalem's Great Synagogue and demanded the resignation of religious party ministers from the Cabinet: they recited psalms in memory of the massacred Palestinians. But by and large the division was along racial, not political or religious, lines; this division has always existed in the background, but the war has projected it into the open, and into Israeli partisan politics.

The final moral loss concerned the armed forces. By obeying the politicians' orders the IDF came to feel it had lost its 'purity of arms' and the forces' reputation had been besmirched, in its own eyes and in the eyes of the world.

It might be thought that all these losses would have transformed the thinking of Israeli expansionists on the subject of Greater Israel. Even the first step, the absorption of southern Lebanon, has proved more difficult than was at first thought. But the expansionist ideas remain. In the first fortnight of October, Sharon made several statements claiming that Jordan, which he calls 'the Palestinian state', comprised 70% to 75% of the Land of Israel, or Eretz Israel (*The Times,* 13 October). Since the central belief of Zionism is the recovery of all of Eretz Israel for the Jewish people, clearly for such people as Sharon so large a part cannot be permanently renounced. For such Israelis the map presented to the Versailles Conference is still on the table.

Despite all the criticism of the war, and of Begin and Sharon, inside and outside Israel, 'the first survey of public opinion [in Israel] since the Beirut massacres has demonstrated clearly that the Prime Minister and his Defence Minister remain far and away the most popular politicians in the country, despite a slight denting in their lead' (Christopher Walker, *The Times,* 30 September).

Approval of Begin's performance dropped from 82% to 72% and Sharon's from 78% to 64%. Thus, their base of support in their real constituency, the Sephardi community — now a majority in Israel — remained intact, enabling them to win again in any general election in the near future.

Menachem Begin is a politician of unusual consistency, a quality rarely displayed by politicians. On 12 October 1955, speaking in the Knesset, he said, 'I deeply believe in launching a preventive war against the Arab States without hesitation. By doing so we will achieve two targets: firstly, the annihilation of Arab power, and, secondly, the expansion of our own territory.' On 8 August 1982, 27 years later, Begin answered criticisms that he had launched Israel into its first aggressive war. Talking to officers of the National Defence College (*Jerusalem Post,* international edition, 22–28 August), he said that of Israel's five wars two were 'wars without an alternative', that is, defensive wars imposed on Israel: these were the 'War of Independence' in 1947-49 and the Yom Kippur War of 1973. The other three were wars of Israel's choice, the Suez War (1956), the Six-Day War (1967) and the 'Peace for Galilee' operation.

He argued that the wars of choice were preferable to those without an alternative because they caused fewer casualties. This was a remarkable confession, because as recently as 4 September in a letter to President Reagan he had said that the 1967 war was 'forced' on Israel. A month later he was saying, 'We must be honest with ourselves. We decided to attack him [Nasser].' And on the 1982 war: 'the terrorists did not threaten the existence of the State of Israel'.

Begin drew this conclusion: 'there is no divine mandate to go to war only when there is no alternative'; what is really important is 'that the price of victory will be few casualties, not many'. In short, Israel has attacked before and will attack again for the purpose, among others, of saving the lives of its soldiers. And Israel will have to attack again – in seven years' time, according to General Ben Gal.

But that is only one camp in Israel. Another is reflected in the text of the Dry Bones cartoon in the *Jerusalem Post* (international edition, 26 September –2 October): 'When terrorists attacked from Syria we blamed the Syrians. When murderous infiltrators slipped in from Lebanon we blamed the Lebanese. When PLO killers launched raids from Jordan we blamed the Jordanians. When Fedayeen goons came in from Egypt we blamed the Egyptians. But when we send a bloodthirsty gang into a refugee camp we blame everyone in the world except ourselves. Whether it was omission or commission we've got something to atone for this Yom Kippur!'

Chronology

June–September 1982

6 June	Israel invades Lebanon.
7 June	Tyre falls.
8 June	Sidon falls.
9 June	Damour falls; Israel attacks Syrian Sam missiles.
14 June	Israel's encirclement of Beirut complete.
20 June	Begin visits Washington.
25 June	Haig resigns as Secretary of State; Shultz succeeds him in July.
3 July	Estimated 100,000 Israelis demonstrate in Tel-Aviv against the war.
4 July	Israel cuts off water and electricity to West Beirut.
9 July	Syria refuses to take any PLO guerrillas who leave Beirut (but later changes its mind).
20 July	Saudi and Syrian foreign ministers visit Washington.
25 July	Arafat signs the 'McCloskey paper' accepting UN resolutions on Palestine.
1 August	The fourth, and heaviest, phase of the bombardment of Beirut begins.
2 August	Reagan sends birthday greetings to Begin.
10 August	Agreement is reached on the Habib plan (after more than a month of haggling).
12 August	After the heaviest bombardment of the war, the siege of Beirut ends.
21 August	PLO evacuation from Beirut begins.
23 August	Bashir Gemayel elected Lebanon's president.

1 September	Reagan launches a new Middle East peace initiative; Israel rejects it.
9 September	Arab summit at Fez puts forward a new Arab peace plan.
14 September	Assassination of president-elect Gemayel in a Beirut explosion.
15 September	Israeli forces move into West Beirut.
16–18 September	Massacre of Palestinians at refugee camps of Sabra and Shatilla, in Beirut.
21 September	Election of Amin Gemayel as Lebanese president.